YIPPEE IN MY SOUL!

by Margaret Bonnette
with Ed Erny

Published by
OMS International
Box A
Greenwood, Indiana 46142-6599

CONTENTS

CONTENTS Continued

FOREWORD

Laugh and cry with Margaret Bonnette as she shares 20 years of Haiti medical missionary adventure with you. This is a book you will not want to put down until you have read it all.

Who says missionaries can't live thrilling lives? Who says that you ever get accustomed to the tragedies, the poverty, and the pathetic needs of a hurting people? Who says that you are robbed of the joy of living and serving Jesus when you face the haunting spiritual darkness, the demon-driven voodooists stalking your way, and when you live with repeated physical danger?

Margaret Bonnette proves to you that 20 years of identifying with the poverty and the needs of Haiti, 20 years of escapes and escapades, 20 years of ministering to the poorest of the poor in remote mountain villages need never rob you of the zest for living and serving. It need not deprive you of the joy of the Lord. You can still have the hallelujah "yippee" in your soul!

Margaret captivates you as she leads you from one short chapter to another. You cringe with her from festering abscesses and machete wounds. You rejoice with her at the transformation Jesus brings in lives and at the integrity of simple born-again believers.

Margaret did not choose to live in the safety and comparative comfort of a missionary center. She was inwardly drawn by the Spirit to where only pioneering spirits could be content, where poverty and demonic darkness combined in its most needy and crude forms, and where missionary living offers a very simple yet very satisfying life.

Whether digging maggots from festering feet or kicking rats from off the bed, whether exhausted from climbing trails or straddling wooden saddles till she was sore, whether dodging Haitian bullets or gunning the sturdy pickup over bumpy ground to escape pursuing mobsters, or whether standing in the rain to wash off perspiration and grime--Margaret never lost her joyous laugh, her singing heart, her gusto, or her holy "yippee!" You will find it to the very last sentence of her book.

Missionaries come in delightful sorts and styles. God makes to order their personalities for the ministry to which He calls them. God knew what He was doing when He prepared and called Margaret Bonnette to Haiti, to the end-of-the-road villages along the northern coast. God enabled her to survive and thrive in spite of pressure, dangerous agitation and budding terrorists, and in spite of the most primitive conditions for living, travel, and service.

Loved by her co-workers, beloved by her Haitian people, and smiled upon by her faithful God, she pressed on heroically. Read all about it in these captivating chapters.

The history of OMS International in Haiti is the taking over of a small radio station and a handful of Haitian co-workers and expanding it across northern Haiti down to the capital city of Port-au-Prince. It is a story of evangelistic teams, of laymen, of church planting, of a vocational Bible school to train Haitian youth for serving their Lord and their people, of a central clinic serving people from a wide area, and radio ministry daily in French, Creole, English, and Spanish, reaching out to Haiti and the surrounding islands from Cuba in the west, to the Bahamas in the north, and the Caicos and Turks Islands in the east.

Let Margaret Bonnette illustrate for you how God uses His servants, provides for their needs, guides their ministry, anoints them day by day, and meets the needs of those for whom Christ died.

Wesley L. Duewel
President-Emeritus,
OMS International

Chapter One

What Am I Doing Here?

"Lord, what am I doing in this airplane at 30,000
feet and headed for the little country of Haiti? Have I
read you wrong, Lord? If so, just turn this airplane
around and head me right back to the United States."

These are some of the thoughts I found running
through my mind that December day in 1965 as I flew
over the cobalt-blue Caribbean waters. God had called
me to be a missionary three-and-a-half years ago. There
was no question about that, but now with my homeland
receding and the gulf between me and my daughter
growing wider by the minute, doubts assailed me. Was
this the right time? the right place? Here I was a widow
turning my back on home, security, and all that was
familiar and leaving Sydney, my lovely 19-year-old
daughter, more precious than life to me, just as she was
entering college. If she had problems and needed me,
where would I be? Practically on another planet. "Oh
God, search me right to the bottom of my heart and soul
I pray. I throw myself at your mercy."

"What Am I Doing Here?"

The crumb of land emerging from the misty waters of the Caribbean was Haiti. In the months since I learned that my mission, The Oriental Missionary Society, was sending me to Haiti (not Ecuador as I had originally thought) I had tried to learn as much as I could about this tragic island.

Haiti means "high ground" in the language of the Arawak Indians, the island's original inhabitants. This name derives from the fact that the topography is dominated by two mountain chains that stretch like long, gnarled arms across the country's northern and southern peninsulas.

About the size of the state of Maryland, Haiti is the western one-third of the once fabled island of Hispanola, discovered by Columbus in 1492. The Dominican Republic comprises the eastern two-thirds of the island.[1]

In the first free election in the history of the nation, in 1957, a tough, rough-hewn country doctor by the name of Francois Duvalier was elected president. By 1964 Duvalier had attained such total control of Haiti, he brazenly declared himself president for life. That December afternoon when my plane approached the capitol city of Port-au-Prince, the island of Haiti was firmly in the cruel, greedy, tyrannical grasp of President Francois Duvalier, known to everyone as Papa Doc. The

---

[1]For more of the history of Haiti, see appendix.

9

economy was so crippled that per capita income was reduced to little more than $300 a year. Due to the poor diet, primitive and unsanitary living conditions, infant mortality rate stood at 60%. The average life span was hardly 40 years. Illiteracy was 92%.

As the aircraft descended I surveyed the scene taking shape before my eyes. Mountains surrounding the capitol city, once verdant with lush forests, had long since been denuded of trees. Brown and seared in the withering heat, the sight of them added to the heaviness of my spirit. "This is nothing like America," I thought. "Lord, what am I doing in a place like this?"

Port-au-Prince, the capital city of nearly one million, possesses beautiful boulevards and fine residential districts where Haiti's elite, wealthy French and mulattoes, live in elegant mansions. For the most part, however, the city is a depressing tangle of shabby, nondescript buildings, disreputable stucco and cement block structures, mud huts, even shanties erected amid mountains of fetid refuse, providing meager shelter for thousands of Haitian peasants who flood into the capital in desperate search for some means of subsistence.

Port-au-Prince has one of the world's few capital city airports that is still not air-conditioned. The muggy, oppressive heat, the congested baggage claim area where a melee of passengers scramble for belongings or argue belligerently with customs inspectors, make for a crude reception for the North American traveler forced now to emerge from the color coordinated air-conditioned womb of a Pan Am 747. I'd lived in many U.S. cities, but never in the old South. For a moment I felt strangely disoriented as though I had been unceremoniously plunked on a foreign planet. I, and a few other white passengers, were fully enveloped by a black sea of humanity. I scanned the faces looking disconcertedly for the missionaries I had been assured would meet my plane. At last, with a sigh of relief I spotted two likely candidates. I made my way over to them. "You must be from OMS," I said with a sigh of relief. "Yes, we're Marilyn and Ina. You must be Margaret Bonnette."

Chapter Two

JOURNEY TO VAUDREUIL

That night we stayed at the Hotel Plaza, and the next morning headed for the local "greyhound" station to catch our bus to Cap Haitien in the north, where the OMS center is located. "This bus ride may not be like anything you've ever experienced before," Ina warned.

Soon I caught sight of the outlandish conveyance that was to be our home for the next ten hours, a trip that would have taken no more than three hours in the States. The so called "bus" was just a truck cab with a huge box bolted to the chassis. The rough wooden seats were designed for two but could, I discovered, be made to accommodate four passengers if properly wedged in, along with infants squalling and squirming on their mothers' laps. Yet these vehicles are a marvelous exhibit of indigenous art. Painted vivid colors, the side panels were embellished with Biblical scenes. One depicted the nativity with Joseph, Mary and a haloed Baby Jesus under a thatched roof. Another portrayed the ascension with Jesus rising beatifically into a multi-colored cloud. Still another showed David and Goliath. Bible verses were emblazoned without apology on front and back. My favorites were "Jesus loves you," "Jesus will return," "Jesus saves" and "The Lord is my Shepherd." Of course all were written in Creole which the girls translated for me.

With a long blast of the horn we were off on what would be a day-long journey over rugged dirt or cobblestone roads. We lurched and swayed through miles of sugar cane fields, bananas groves, or along barren stretches of the island coast where rugged mountains sloped down to the sea. As we passed through the verdant rice belt section I wondered how Haitians could work so many hours in the water, transplanting the small bundles of rice seedlings by hand. I remembered warnings about leeches and other parasites which latch onto legs or enter body openings to wreak all sorts of havoc.

As the bus swayed and lurched around curves or bumped mercilessly over washed-out sections of the road, we passengers were thrown unceremoniously from side to side. I found myself continually hanging on to anything, or anyone, for dear life. Five hours into the journey we reached the half-way point where the bus stopped and disgorged its human cargo for a few moments respite to stretch and relieve ourselves. I was shocked to see the men casually standing along the side of the bus urinating, without a thought of anyone watching. Fortunately, we managed to find an alleyway that protected us from curious onlookers.

It was all I could do to make myself crawl back into

that bus. I picked my way through an obstacle course just to get back to my assigned seat. Live chickens and bags of all sizes were situated just where one's feet should be. One chicken bit me as I passed. I told the owner a thing or two, but knew I was safe since she didn't understand English.

The last portion of the journey took us over steep mountain terrain. No roller coaster was more up and down and curvy than that road for the next 75 miles. My missionary tour guides kept me entertained, showing me where busses had gone over the side, plunging into the ravines below. This didn't help stem the tide of apprehension rising steadily inside of me.

Finally we came to the old French plantation gate that led to the OMS compound and the radio station I had heard so much about. Radio 4VEH, the evangelical voice of Haiti, had been founded in 1954 by an intrepid visionary named G.T. Bustin. The only Christian radio station in northern Haiti, 4VEH had developed a huge listening audience in the Cap Haitien area, and its signal reached throughout the islands of the Caribbean as well as Central America and portions of South America. In 1957, at Bustin's request, the struggling 4VEH work was assumed by The Oriental Missionary Society. Three missionaries who had been with 4VEH from the beginning joined OMS. They were radio engineer Mardy Picazo and his talented wife, Rachel, along with Aldean Saufley, the station announcer and an enormously gifted musician. Under OMS's sponsorship the work of 4VEH expanded to include the planting of churches, a vocational Bible school for training of pastors and evangelists, and medical and dental clinics. OMS's MFM (Men For Missions) volunteers by the score had come to the field to construct churches, nine missionary residences, the vocational Bible school and the clinic. They also erected a new radio tower, and replaced the all-but-defunct 4VEH transmitters. Many of these MFM laymen stayed on to become career missionaries. In time Haiti boasted more OMS missionaries than any other of the mission's ten fields.

When I arrived, there were 14 missionaries resident at our mission center at Vaudreuil. The staff included six single women. Three of them worked in the radio station; Flo Boyer, a nurse who had founded the clinic was on furlough. The nurse, Jan Elam, whom I was to replace was scheduled to leave in a few weeks.

When we arrived at the gate of the compound we were none too sorry to be rid of that colorful old bus. We emerged looking like cripples. I'd been scrunched up for so many hours that I could hardly stand or walk straight. It took two days to recover from the sore muscles and bruises I acquired on that journey.

Much as I appreciated the delegation of missionaries that were on hand to greet the new nurse, all I could think of at that moment was a bed and a good night's sleep. I praised the Lord for a safe trip, thinking that my guardian angels must be as exhausted as I was.

My housing assignment was the old wood-framed

house where five other single lady missionaries lived. In its heyday a century earlier, it had been a mansion housing the French owners of the plantation on which property the mission compound had been built. In the intervening years, time, termites and an assortment of pests had done their work. That house had a menagerie all its own, which included rats, mice, cockroaches, and bedbugs. I never will forgive the dirty rat that ate the top out of one of my shoes. But the bedbugs were by far the greatest problem. I was there only a week before I followed the example of the other ladies, taking my mattress and springs outside to paint them with a mixture of mothballs and kerosene. I've never liked the smell of mothballs, but that was preferable to bugs and bed mates! As I eased my weary body into my bed that night the uncertainty and questions of the day before had been replaced by a deep settled peace. Already I was sensing a tremendous surge of love for the Haitian people welling up from deep within my being. It is a love which I never lost and came as a confirmation of God's seal upon my call to Haiti. And this land so intimidating, so uncomfortable yesterday, was already beginning to feel like home. It was my "promised land" in a very real sense. I could have knelt down and kissed it. Yes, there was peace in my heart and I knew I was exactly where God wanted me. I had come a long way from those early years in Oklahoma.

Chapter Three

A Kid From Oklahoma

I was born in Broken Bow, Oklahoma, a small town in the mountainous, wooded Southeastern corner of the state. My parents were Harvey and Mary Wooden. They had met and married while still in high school. "Much too young," mother would sometimes lament with a note of warning in her voice.

Dad had made a success of his lumber business, and his mill in time employed more than 100 men, 80 of them black. We had a happy home and my childhood memories are good ones, although religion was regarded as a superfluous ritual requiring no more than occasional church attendance at Easter and perhaps Christmas. Most of the neighborhood children could be found in Sunday school on a Sabbath morning, but the Wooden kids were not among them.

Though dad was usually stern and businesslike he could be tender. I recall times when he actually said, "I love you, Margaret." It was mother, however, with whom I developed a special bond (and it was she who later came to share my precious faith in the Savior). When people commented that "Margaret really takes after her mother" I was always pleased.

The word "unique" is one of the most overused words in the American vocabulary. But all who knew mother agreed that that word certainly described her. Though she had little schooling, quitting before she had finished high school, she was a woman of boundless energy. With her relentlessly inquisitive mind and irrepressible zest for living she read voraciously, taught herself all kinds of skills from designing clothes to architecture, even designing the home dad built for us. More than this, she had an adventuresome madcap streak that moved her to try all sorts of wild, improbable escapades. This must have been at least, in part, the legacy of her pioneer stock. Yes, to my mother I owe my preference for living in remote, sometimes wild, hinterlands over the comforts and security of city life.

There were four of us Wooden children--three girls and a boy. I arrived first to be followed by Helen, Harvey and Nona.

Although my family ties remain strong to this day, it was mother alone who stood with me in my call to serve Christ as a missionary to Haiti. Dad, who had little love for blacks, was baffled and angry that his daughter who could "make great money in nursing" would do such a fool, stupid thing as to go off and waste her life among illiterate natives who would never appreciate her anyway!

A Kid From Oklahoma

I lost a dear friend when my mother died in 1966, just a few months after I arrived in Haiti. Though many witnessed to dad, he, as far as I know, died an unbeliever in 1971.

Helen and her husband who made their home in Wright City, Oklahoma, were tragically killed in an automobile accident in 1991. Today Nona and her husband live in Wynnewood, Oklahoma, and Harvey in Louisville, Kentucky.

Following graduation from high school in 1941 I enrolled in the University of Oklahoma where I planned to major in biology with a view to taking up the nursing profession. With the Japanese attack on Pearl Harbor December 7 of that year our nation was suddenly at war. In the wake of this tragedy there came tremendous upheavals in American society, as our boys mobilized for what was to be the greatest conflict in the history of the world. With all the excitement came unprecedented job opportunities for women as a result of the war effort. It was no time for me to be wasting my life in an obscure backwater like the University of Oklahoma I decided. So when a girlfriend urged me to go with her to California where her brother promised all sorts of exciting jobs I was ready. We quit school in February and by June I had a job with the IMAC Radar Tube Company located in San Bruno, California, just 15 miles south of San Francisco, a city teeming with handsome young men in uniform.

Sailors and GIs were everywhere and shyness has never been one of my characteristics. I loved dancing and had no trouble making friends. Soon my social calendar was more than full. I told myself it was my patriotic duty to "make all the boys happy." With ships and planes departing daily for the front there was a poignant, bittersweet quality in the air. The whirlwind romance was the norm. It was a time to, as the poet said, "gather ye rosebuds while ye may."

As a result I did something that even for me, headstrong and impulsive as I was, and am, seems quite incredible. To this day I blush to think about it. I became engaged to two servicemen at once. I was convinced I loved them both, reasoning that war, being what it is, chances are only one of them would return.

Now lest you think that this period of my life was all giddiness and frivolity I should tell you that at the IMAC Radar Tube Company my hard work and conscientious efforts were not going unnoticed. In time I was promoted to the research lab although I had no formal training for this kind of work. I found I was gifted with a creative and analytical mind and as a result I was credited with two inventions.

Circumstances which led to my meeting Virgil Bonnette, Jr., my future husband, were peculiar to say the least. Virgil, who actually came from our same "neck of the woods" in Southeastern Oklahoma, had graduated from the University of Oklahoma with a degree in chemical engineering. During college he had joined the NROTC and following commencement was assigned to the destroyer U.S.S. Norman Scott and went directly to war. In those early naval battles in '42 and '43 the U.S. fleet had not recovered from the Pearl Harbor disaster and was often badly out-manned by ships of the Japanese Imperial Navy. In 1943 Virgil's ship got into a fierce skirmish in the battle of Siapan and Tinian. The U.S.S. Norman Scott was shot up badly, the whole topside blown away, and Virgil was wounded.

When the ship returned to San Francisco the wounded were the first to get leave. Virgil soon found himself back in Oklahoma enjoying his status as a decorated war hero. There on the streets of the city one afternoon he met my father and an uncle with my little sister Nona in tow. When Virgil mentioned that he would be shipping out of San Francisco Nona squealed "Oh, my sister lives near San Francisco. You ought to meet her!" When Virgil expressed some mild interest Nona impulsively dashed home, returning with sister Margaret's address and phone number--both her home phone and office phone! And that is how one September day in 1943 I picked up the phone and found myself talking to a charming masculine voice belonging to one Lt. Virgil Bonnette, Jr..

Unaccountably I found myself excited, very excited, inappropriately excited for a girl already engaged. I did something I'd never done before. I asked my boss for the day off agreeing to meet Virgil at the St. Francis Hotel in San Francisco.

When I first spotted him, tall, handsome, immaculately uniformed, approaching me across the hotel

Yippee in my Soul!

lobby my heart leaped. It was really love at first sight. We were married six weeks later. Now I faced the painful task of writing not one but two "Dear John" letters. The first gentleman accepted this dismaying turn of events with resignation, but with the second one it was a different story. The moment he set foot on shore he headed for my apartment in a rage. "I oughta kill you," he roared, and for a moment I thought he would.

Chapter Four

Back Of The Clouds

After V-J Day we located at Niagara Falls, N.Y., where Virgil took up his profession as a chemical engineer with The Olin-Mathison Company. A short time later I gave birth to a beautiful baby girl. We named her Sydney.

Virgil elected to remain in the Naval Reserves never dreaming how soon he would be called up. But with the outbreak of the Korean War in June 1950 he again found himself in Naval uniform. Surprisingly his ship was not dispatched to Asian waters but rather to the Mediterranean. Due to his background in chemical engineering, however, he was eventually assigned to the Naval Research Center in Dahlgren, Virginia, and promoted to the rank of Full Commander. A year earlier he and seven other men had developed a jet fuel, hydrozine. He also attempted, without success, to perfect a liquid explosive suitable for use in firearms.

With the war over, future prospects seemed rosy. Virgil's income was sufficient to afford a beautiful home and just about anything our hearts desired. Sydney, our beautiful daughter, was the sunshine of our home and the joy of our lives.

Then, imperceptibly at first, our horizons began to darken. The first small cloud appeared in the form of annoying polyps in Virgil's nose. "Nothing to worry about," the doctor assured him. "They can be surgically removed." Thus began twelve years of surgery. The polyps, eventually diagnosed as cancerous, cropped up with increasing and alarming regularity in his nose, spreading, in time, to the sinus cavities. When surgery failed to eliminate the growths, radiation treatment was begun. The cancer, he was finally informed, was spreading towards the brain. The final nine and a half months were for Virgil an ordeal of excruciating pain, so intense at times that even drugs did not bring relief. I was seized with growing anxiety which escalated to panic and horror as I stood by helplessly, wishing somehow I could share the physical torment of this man I loved.

Now as though the drama of our lives was being orchestrated by some malevolent unseen force, we were dealt another blow. I discovered large lumps on both of Sydney's legs. A medical examination revealed bone tumors. What more could possibly go wrong? I thought, as I struggled out of bed those bleak mornings.

Little did I guess that our Lord, in a supreme act of love, was dealing me what C.S. Lewis would term a "severe mercy." I know now that nothing short of affliction would have served to get our attention in our headlong plunge into a life of selfish obsession with our own plans, all calculated to bring us prosperity and pleasure by the barrelful. Affliction was beginning to bear its divinely appointed fruit in my life. Now I know so well what the psalmist meant when he said, "Before I was afflicted I went astray, but now I have kept Thy Word."

The first token of God's divine initiative came when Sydney returned from Sunday school one morning to announce that she had asked Jesus into her heart. Her pure, innocent joy struck a deep responsive cord in my heart. More than this, surgery on her legs was successful and the tumors proved benign.

Among my acquaintances there was one woman who clearly had something I lacked--a serenity and inner glow, a joy that did not stem from the latest cocktail party or house full of expensive furnishings. Her name was Ida Putnam. She was a Christian. I knew I had to talk to Ida Putnam.

Ida gave me a Bible with the instructions, "Read any part of it you want, but be sure to read the Gospel of John. Keep reading John." She clearly understood the purpose for which the fourth Gospel was inspired--a purpose explained by the beloved apostle in Chapter 20:31, "These things are written that ye might believe that Jesus is the Christ the Son of God, and that believing ye might have life in His name."

It was not long before I realized that I held in my hand a treasure. I marveled that I had lived 33 years without ever entering the precincts of Holy Scripture. I read with ever-increasing thirst the Old Testament, the New, but always coming back to John.

Two weeks after Ida Putnam put that Bible in my hands she moved to Connecticut, but she had left with me the Book that would change my life. As I immersed myself in Scripture the divine light began to break into my tragic, darkened world. A new day was dawning and though no outward circumstances changed and my husband seemed doomed by the curse of cancer, there crept daily into my heart sweet, pervasive, inexplicable peace--the peace that Jesus gives. One March afternoon in 1959 I knelt by my bed and asked Jesus Christ to occupy the throne of my life.

Though I hardly knew how to break the news to my dying husband, he sensed immediately that something had happened. We began to read the Scriptures together. Praise God, five days before Virgil died he received Jesus Christ as his Savior.

Even today I can remember the sense of amazement that possessed me after Virgil's passing. The dark, terrible torment that I thought would annihilate me had instead forced me to plunge into the fountain of eternal life. I'd emerged from the greatest loss a human being can sustain, not destroyed and broken, but a new woman with a whole new life before me, charged with excitement that I would enter every day for the rest of my life with Jesus by my side. His Holy Spirit, the sweet Comforter, was within guiding, encouraging, instructing.

Chapter Five

Beginning Again

I moved with Sydney to Sebring, Florida, a city I had previously visited where I had been impressed by the friendly community. I found a job working as a dental assistant doing everything from taking and developing x-rays to billing customers. We began attending the Sebring First United Methodist Church pastored by Rev. Clarence Yates. Under his inspired preaching and rich exposition of the Word I began to grow, at the same time finding opportunity for Christian service within the context of that fine church. More than this, Clarence and his wife, Charlotte, became invaluable friends and counselors, greatly used of God to steady my first faltering footsteps in a walk of faith which would lead eventually to my call to missions and Haiti.

Unaccountably there came within my heart a growing conviction that God wanted me to be a missionary. That seems all the stranger now in that as a new Christian I had virtually no contact with missions or missionaries, the single exception being a dull,

Yippee in my Soul!

unattractive missionary lady of the "old school" who had come to our church. She did anything but inspire one to join her in that "joyless" profession.

One August evening in 1961 I came home from the dental clinic unusually tired with a growing and very disturbing feeling that God was speaking to me and the subject was missions. I hastily prepared supper and then exhausted threw myself on the bed and poured out my heart to God.

Then in the semi-darkness of that room I suddenly became conscious of the presence of two heavenly beings. Though I heard no audible voice I knew with absolute certainty that they were speaking God's message to me, and that message was a simple one. God was indeed calling me to be a missionary.

These angelic beings did not appear, as they often do in a light of overwhelming brightness, yet their forms were clearly visible to me in the half-darkness of my room although their features were barely discernable. How I knew with such certainty that these emissaries had been sent from God I can hardly tell except to say they exuded a divine sense of well-being, like a heavenly benediction quelling any natural human fear.

Me a missionary? I thought. That's preposterous! Lord, what qualifications do I have? And what about Sydney now in high school? How could I leave her? I have since learned that once God has spoken there is no use arguing or equivocating. His will was clear and His will was good--nothing short of the best. That was that and it was time to put my life in order and prepare to be a missionary.

Since my first abortive start at the University of Oklahoma I had made several desultory attempts to continue my formal education. While living in Niagara Falls, N.Y., I'd actually enrolled twice in the university and had on another occasion taken several courses by correspondence, including archaeology and conchology--the study of shells. My early girlhood dream, however, had been to become a nurse. Now it was time to make that dream come true for the glory of Jesus Christ. We moved to Tampa, found an apartment and I entered the school of nursing. One of my teachers, a godly evangelical woman, upon learning that I was preparing for medical missions, went out of her way to encourage me, even giving me private instruction in tropical medicine. In the years ahead how grateful I would be for what she taught me.

Chapter Six

"Get To Know Those People From OMS"

With the completion of my nursing degree and Sydney's pending graduation from high school, two questions faced us. To what country was I to go as a missionary and with what organization? And where was Sydney to go to college?

Clarence and Charlotte Yates were God's special agents of guidance at this time. Clarence's classmate at Asbury College had been a winsome, charismatic personality named Bill Gillam. Bill had served as a missionary for years in Colombia, South America, and was then vice-president of homeland ministries with The Oriental Missionary Society.

"Margaret," Clarence told me that winter of 1964, "OMS is having a convention at St. Petersburg. I want you to go. Check out this organization. Get to know their people and meet my friend Bill Gillam. You'll like him."

When the OMS convention opened in St. Pete the

next month I arrived on the scene a total stranger. I didn't know a soul and no one in OMS had ever heard of Margaret Bonnette, a forty-one year old soon-to-be-graduated nurse, who was sure God wanted her to be a missionary.

Somewhat intimidated I entered the big auditorium and found a seat well towards the rear. As the service progressed the joyful, inspired music, testimonies from radiant missionaries and laymen, and the gripping address transported me. I could feel a tingling warmth move up my spine and into every nerve of my body vibrating with excitement. These are my kind of people I repeated to myself over and over.

After the service I looked for Bill Gillam. When I located him he was surrounded, as always, by a cluster of friends. There was a warmth and joy just being in the presence of this man. Shyly I waited my turn, screwing up my courage and rehearsing the speech I was going to make. Finally when the crowd had dispersed he turned to me with a broad smile.

"You don't know me," I began hesitantly, "but I'm Margaret Bonnette and your friend Clarence Yates is my pastor. God has called me to be a missionary nurse. I wonder if OMS has a place for me."

Before the evening was over I had learned a lot about OMS, an organization begun by Charles and Lettie Cowman in 1901, and known for its strategy of training nationals, planting indigenous churches, and organizing

Yippee in my Soul!

Every Creature Crusades to put Scriptures in every home of a nation. Bill told me that there was indeed an immediate need for a missionary nurse in Ecuador where the mission had a clinic for Saraguro Indians high in the Andes.

The next day I wrote OMS President Dr. Eugene Erny of my intentions. His reply came informing me that since I was 41, six years over the age limit for regular missionaries, I would at first be accepted by OMS as an associate missionary working under OMS auspices, entirely responsible for my own support and financial needs. And, oh yes, rather than go to Ecuador, would I consider going to Haiti, since Flora Boyer, the nurse who had founded the clinic, was on a year's furlough, and the other nurse was making plans to return to the U.S.

So there was a critical need in Haiti for some trained medical person to run the clinic. I was being perceived as this person and that realization petrified me. The prospect of taking charge of the clinic was terrifying to say the least. But God, who had called me to serve Him in a foreign country, had not only opened the door He had flung it practically off its hinges. A fresh-from-nurses training, untried, unproven, green as green can be, neophyte in charge of a clinic! All I could say was, "Lead on, O King Eternal."

The one anxiety remaining was Sydney. Since Virgil's death this precious daughter of mine had been my companion, the focus of my pride, her smile lighting each day. We were more than mother and daughter, more than dear friends. Our lives had been sweetly melded together, first through sorrow and then through the joy of new life in Jesus. I could hardly bear the thought of leaving her, especially at this critical, so-vulnerable time in her life, as she graduated from high school and entered as a freshman the daunting and dangerous world of the college campus. Again God used Clarence and Charlotte Yates to guide me to their alma mater. "Why not take Sydney to the campus for Asbury's homecoming week," they suggested. "Our daughter Sharon is there and she'll show you around and introduce Sydney to some of the kids."

Asbury was God's answer for Sydney and me. It was love at first sight. The beautiful campus of Asbury College with its picturesque, columned buildings is nestled in the heart of the blue grass, just a few minutes south of Kentucky's cultural center of Lexington. Everyone we met was so friendly that we left with a deep conviction that Asbury was indeed God's place for Sydney. Now my heart was at rest. I packed for Haiti knowing Sydney would be at a school sanctified by the prayers of God's people; she would be instructed by wise, godly professors and surrounded by young people with a sincere commitment to the will of God. And it was on that campus that she would meet and fall in love with the young man she was destined to share her life with.

Ah, yes, Lord, I thought as I drifted off to slumber in that termite-ridden, old plantation house in Vaudreuil, You've brought me a long way, but I have a feeling that the best is still ahead.

Chapter Seven

"How Will I Ever Manage?"

I will never forget my first day in the clinic--a simple cement block building consisting of three examining rooms and a lab. OMS would later build a large, well-furnished clinic, but in 1965 the work was only a few years old and strictly a "one-horse affair."

Jan Elam, the nurse I was replacing, showed me around, giving me an impromptu briefing. To my amazement and horror I learned that my assignment was not to be nursing at all. Instead, I was expected to consult, diagnose and prescribe--the work of an M.D.--the very thing they had told me in nursing school that I must never, never do! "Lord," I cried inwardly, "how will I ever manage this?"

After a few days I was given an interpreter and put on my own. Jan informed me that she'd soon be leaving Haiti and must busy herself with packing, last farewells, etc., but not to worry she'd stop by every now and then to see how I was doing. After one week she was satisfied that I could manage on my own. "You're doing fine,

Margaret," she said. "I'll plan to leave in five days." Those last five days I became that woman's shadow, following her wherever she went, asking questions, observing procedures and treatments and making notes. I'll be forever indebted to Jan for patiently shepherding me through those first frightening days of my "baptism of fire."

The day before Jan left we decided to walk to the city of Cap Haitien, five miles away. It was fun to stroll along and greet everyone we passed. The Haitians are such friendly people, and by then I could at least say "Bonjour, koman ou ye?" (Good day, how are you?) and respond to their greetings with "Mouin bein merci" (I'm fine, thanks).

Every once in a while we'd stop at a roadside stand to buy a banana, orange or a delicious deep-fried delicacy. The fruit which could be peeled was germ free, and the snacks if freshly cooked and untouched by human hands were safe as well.

We spent at least two hours just walking around the city. Then it was time to return to the compound. About halfway back we felt an urgent need for a restroom and started looking for some bushes or trees, safely removed from inquisitive eyes, to serve our purpose. It wasn't easy as there seemed to be people everywhere. Finally we located some shrubs growing a short distance from the road, which seemed to afford some privacy. A few minutes later I looked up to find about eight bemused Haitians standing about thirty feet from us looking on. I didn't know Creole and knew they didn't understand English. "Yes, we're white all over," I blurted out. Jan burst out laughing as did the spectators.

Though I would be given opportunity for formal language study later, during these early months I had to flounder along learning as much Creole as I could on my own. At this time, although the official language of Haiti was French, it was spoken mainly by the "haute bourgeoisie," the elite governing class, consisting primarily of French and mulattoes who lived, for the most part, in Port-au-Prince. Everyone else spoke Creole. Creole is a sort of corrupted French that resulted when African slaves came to Haiti and began trying to speak the French language. Though essentially of French derivation Creole preserves the phonetic habits and grammatical structure of African tongues, particularly the dialects of Dahomey and Nigeria, areas of Africa from which most Haitians slaves came. I could find only one little booklet telling foreigners how to speak the Creole language. I carried it around wherever I went those first weeks, and also had a Haitian boy to help me identify things when I went outside the compound. It was a beginning but, oh, how much I had to learn.

Chapter Eight

Every Disease Imaginable

It wasn't long before things were in full swing for me at the clinic. Most of our patients were peasants who lived in the most appalling circumstances, their homes a one-roomed mud thatch hut, surrounded by filth, refuse and raw sewage. Illiterate, bereft of even rudimentary education, they were prisoners of ignorance, superstition and poverty.

Few of us who come from the Western world can imagine the degree of suffering endured by people in a backward impoverished nation. When we have pain, a headache, or backache we take an aspirin. Haitians don't even have an aspirin. We have a whole medicine cabinet full of medication and access to the best physicians and hospitals in the world. A slight fever or the pain of an ingrown toenail, and we're practically in hysterics, demanding that a doctor attend to us and our pain be promptly alleviated. Because Haitians have none of these blessings they develop an amazing fortitude. They can take pain that would drive most of us up a wall. I was in awe of these simple people who daily demonstrated a kind of courage that has almost disappeared in the West.

The OMS clinic had been founded by my indefatigable predecessor Flo Boyer in response to the appalling need on every side. With pastor Napo Etienne helping, she began treating patients under a mango tree on the OMS compound. Later a 10 x 10 one-room clinic was built, a sheet dividing the consulting and examining areas. Water was carried by hand and a small hot plate used to sterilize needles. Later a more commodious and substantial structure was erected by OMS Men For Missions builders.

Daily I found myself treating every kind of disease imaginable. Many patients complained of "umba ke," which literally means "under the heart." This is actually heartburn or indigestion, the result of lack of food, a diet consisting of immoderate quantities of hot and spicy food, or of going on a binge and gorging themselves. (Because Haitians seldom have enough to eat and are perpetually hungry, when some food does become available they will eat an entire supply at a sitting, not knowing how long it will be before they see a full meal again.)

The unsanitary conditions in Haiti are exacerbated by a chronic water shortage. Running water is virtually unknown in Haitian peasants' homes, and the precious supply must be carried a great distance. Understandably this discourages bathing or even hand washing. As a result parasites abound and worms of every imaginable type--strongaloid pin worms and especially ascaris. Often it was unnecessary to send a stool specimen to the lab to identify the worm, since the mother would bring a sample with her on a leaf or tell us how many had been passed. Ascaris can be deadly, working their way up into the lungs or brain. Two of our patients died of worms perforating their lungs. I even pulled an ascaris out of a child's nose. Sadly, though we could cure the patient, it was usually just a matter of time before they would reinfect themselves.

Due to the inadequate diet and especially lack of protein, many children suffered from a nutritional deficiency called Kwashaiorkor. My heart would break to see the familiar signs of malnutrition--bloated bellies, rust colored hair, diarrhea, irritability and apathy. At first, we gave the mothers food to take home for their children, but when patients often showed no improvement we discovered that others in the family were eating the food too. After that we began feeding malnourished children at the clinic.

Every day patients arrived at the clinic with all sorts of oozing sores, abscesses and wounds. One man had his ear bitten off in a fight. He arrived at the clinic, ear in hand wanting me to sew it back on. Especially common were machete wounds. Machetes are used for just about everything from preparing a meal to working in the garden or harvesting of bananas, while clinging precariously to the side of a steep mountain. These long knives leave wicked gashes, some accidental, some inflicted in a fight.

Venereal disease is endemic in Haiti. Since it is costly to obtain a marriage license, few Haitian couples are married, and this probably contributes to the wanton promiscuity which is the tendency of all sinful man. The widespread influence of voodoo, the national religion of Haiti, also contributes to the raging sexual immorality. Voodoo ceremonies often involve sexual orgies and thus seem to sanction all manner of licentiousness. Also, because of the abject poverty, there is widespread prostitution of both men and women.

At first most of the VD cases we saw were treatable, although unless we could also treat the contact, the patients would almost always reinfect themselves. Toward the late 70s and early 80s we were baffled by cases that, despite all the usual antibiotics, seem to defy treatment. In time the victim would mysteriously weaken and die. Now of course, we know that we were seeing the onset of the AIDS epidemic. AIDS is presently rampant in Haiti. Though no reliable figures are available, doctors suspect the incidence of HIV infection there to be very nearly the highest in the world. When our clinic doctors recently started to routinely check patients for AIDS, of the first ten examined, nine were infected! Male prostitution abounds and many impoverished men sell themselves to witch doctors for their lascivious use.

Occasionally a patient would be brought to the clinic who was demon possessed. Although I could not always tell if someone was demonized, my colleagues who had lived in Haiti all their lives and had seen plenty of this phenomena recognized it immediately. Even non-Christians knew when someone was demon possessed. Whenever we had situations like that my Haitian colleagues and I would surround the victim holding hands and praying. We would then command the demons to leave in Jesus' name. As the spirits exited the body there would often be terrible convulsions and screaming. When you heard the screaming you knew they were coming out. It was a blood curdling sound. I can still hear those shrieks in my mind. There are Westerners who are skeptical about demon possession, explaining it all simply as some form of mental derangement. One will occasionally even read Christian authors and commentators who explain that the New Testament writers of the Gospels, due to their lack of scientific and medical knowledge, simply ascribed all sorts of mental illnesses to demon possession. Missionaries who have lived for years in foreign lands, however, know it is a stark and terrible reality.[2]

---

[2] For more on voodoo in Haiti, see appendix.

Chapter Nine

"*Lord, Show Me*"

To say that my schedule was full would be an understatement. Many days I would see 100 or more patients at the clinic and then go home to find more congregating in my yard or banging on my door. With my limited nurse's training I had no background or experience to do what I was so audaciously attempting. I'm sure that many times I mis-diagnosed or mis-treated patients, but God was gracious, and all the time I was learning. How I was learning! A great deal of my new knowledge came from treating the sick and from my careful observation and study of each patient. But there were many times during these early years when I was baffled, not knowing what to do, how to proceed. When this happened I would leave the patient, walk over to the cabinet or examining table and ask the Lord for help. "Please, Lord," I cried, "I don't know what to do. You know. Show me." Usually something would suddenly come to mind and I would say, "Yes, that's it. Thank you, Lord."

At the same time I read all the medical books I

could lay my hands on and kept my medical texts at my elbow for quick reference. When visiting doctors came, I questioned them non-stop, prying every bit of useful information I could out of them, watching them work with patients and learning their techniques. I was indebted to a doctor from another mission who taught me to suture. With the frequent machete wounds I got lots of practice and developed a deft hand. The straight, neat scars that remained were testimony to my fancy needlework.

Delivering my first baby was a terrifying experience. The young mother arrived, looking with such naive confidence at this new nurse, I couldn't bring myself to turn her away, and in Haiti losing face can be disastrous. All went well and I don't know who was more proud, the mother or I! I always took special satisfaction in giving the newborns tetanus shots knowing that many babies in Haiti die of tetanus as a result of so-called midwives cutting the umbilical cord with a rusty razor blade or a filthy piece of glass.

No patient felt properly attended to unless he was checked with a stethoscope. As a woman was leaving my consulting room one day I overheard her muttering unhappily to herself. I asked if something was wrong. "You forgot to sonne (listen)," she replied. Whereupon I called her back and listened to her chest. I assured her then that my diagnosis had been correct. She left satisfied. Early on I resolved not to just go through the motions of using the stethoscope, but to really listen. Examining thousands of patients in this way I learned a great deal about the sound of the lungs and heart. This proved to be a tremendous benefit.

After being examined Haitian patients often feel that no matter what the ailment they must have an injection or "piki." To their minds a piki will heal anything from a headache to a bad infection.

Perhaps the greatest limitation of our little clinic in those early days was that we had no inpatient services, no beds. We sent the really serious cases to the government hospital in Cap Haitien five miles away. This was far from ideal, but at least they could get IVs and other services that we could not offer. Often, however, patients were reluctant to go to the government hospital knowing they would have to buy their own medications and pay the dollar fee (more than a full day's wages in Haiti) before they could get out. However, not until Dr. Stafford Bourke arrived at the clinic in 1969 did we begin to provide inpatient care. At first we took one of the mission residences and turned it into a little hospital. When I returned from furlough one year, I was given responsibility for this new service and would divide my time between the hospital and the consulting room where I continued to do the same thing I had done for years.

From time to time I would leave Vaudreuil and hold outstation clinics in our churches located in the mountains or "boonies." With a large box packed full of medicine, a sack lunch, and penny toys for the kids, I travelled by pickup, horseback, motorcycle or foot, depending on the location of the church. I dearly loved this type of ministry in spite of saddle sores and aching feet. The Haitian saddles are made of wood and certainly not designed for comfort. But I learned to place both a blanket and pillow atop the crude frame for a better ride on these forays into the remote areas. My nurse assistant always accompanied me, and anyone else who wanted to go along and help.

With scores of needy, suffering people coming to us daily I asked God to help me see in every one of them not only an opportunity to alleviate their pain, but also to introduce them to the Savior. As I examined them or talked with them about their home situation, I would share my witness. Haitians are easy to talk to about the Lord. There is none of the hesitancy we sometimes feel with Westerners who are sophisticated and easily offended. Haitians, often in tremendous bondage to voodoo and demonic spirits, are very conscious of spiritual realities. Our whole clinic staff talked to almost every patient about Jesus, the One who could give eternal life. They praised God, even shouting for joy, when one of them came into the Kingdom. Now they had hope. Most of them had lived lives so full of grinding poverty and pain that it was a blessing to hear them testify that no matter what happened, even if they died, they would live again and there would be no more hunger, no more suffering.

When patients accepted Christ we would direct them to an evangelical church near their home, writing a note of introduction to give to the pastor. In this way many of these dear people were brought into the body of Christ.

Yippee in my Soul!

After four months, the exhausting clinic routine along with the rounds of house calls began to take its toll. The constant exposure to so much suffering was affecting me emotionally. When I got home at night I would break out in tears, sometimes weeping uncontrollably for hours. Finally, one night I fell on my knees beside my bed and said, "Lord, either make me able to take all of this, or send me back to the States."

The next day around noon I suddenly realized that although I was working under the same conditions it wasn't affecting me as before. That was my answer from the Lord.

After a busy day at the clinic I found it was difficult for me to sit or kneel at night for prayer. Then I hit on an idea. Taking a large cardboard scroll I wrote on it the names of all my family, friends, supporters and other prayer requests. I then tacked it to the ceiling over my bed. The names of all my OMS missionaries' families I pinned on the white curtains near the bed. Now when I came home exhausted, all I had to do was lie down on the bed, look up and pray. If I didn't get through the list one night I'd finish the next. Two of the MKs (missionary kids) decided Aunt Margaret had a good idea and did the same at their home.

All the MKs called me Aunt Margaret. In fact, to MKs all of the adult missionaries are uncles and aunts. How great for these kids to grow up in such a large, loving family while in a foreign land. I always enjoyed the MKs coming to my house. They liked playing with the toys I kept in a large box. There were all sizes of dolls, cars, whistles, books, and puzzles. One doll had a belly button which, when pressed, made one eye wink.

When one of the kids became ill I usually gave the medication by mouth or injection. They always felt better when I crawled into bed with them for awhile or until they fell asleep. Two little MKs were bitten by a rabid cat. The other nurse Flo Boyer and I took turns giving the injections on either side of the stomach. Neither of us wanted to give those shots, and we'd both end up crying as we left their home for they were terrifically painful. Thank God we all survived.

Chapter Ten

To Port-au-Prince

Since French was the official language of Haiti, all OMS missionaries were required to study the language for one year. My missionary friend, Valeene Hayes, and I were sent to Port-au-Prince for language study with a private tutor. Valeene had arrived in Haiti a few years before I did, and we hit it off right away. Sweet and sensitive, Valeene is a marvelously gifted lady who with Aldean Saufley is largely responsible for the music ministry of 4VEH. Since childhood she had been afflicted with a heart condition (the result of rheumatic fever) which often left her weak and incapacitated. I'll tell you more about that later and what the Lord did for Valeene. We stayed in a third floor room of a wooden hotel in the capital city. Access to our quarters involved a climb up some old dark, rickety stairs.

This was during the regime of Francois Duvalier who was the country's president-dictator. The name Papa Doc has become synonymous with the worst sort of tyrannical and brutal dictatorship. Duvalier was elected president in 1956, in what was touted as Haiti's first "truly democratic" election. Unlike former presidents who came largely from Haiti's elite class, Duvalier was a peasant. "A simple country doctor," he loved to call himself, "a man of the people."

Hopes for a fair-minded government, however, were soon dashed when Papa Doc showed himself to be a ruthless dictator. A devotee of black arts he openly practiced voodoo in the palace and had the Haitian flag redesigned to include black, the voodoo color. In 1964 he brazenly dispensed with democracy, declaring himself president for life. When he finally died his effete son Jean Claude, usually called Baby Doc, succeeded him. Under Baby Doc life in Haiti actually improved with some relaxation of the rampant terror that was always a part of the old man's regime.

Haiti had an army, but the president kept his own private secret service militia, the Haitian equivalent of the KGB only much worse. They were called the Ton-Ton Macoutes, a name meaning "bogey man." These young bullies wore dark blue pants, shirts and caps and were generally referred to as the Blue Boys. They kept Haitians in absolute terror since they were a law unto themselves and could get away with almost anything.

While I was in language school a Haitian surgeon told me of some of her encounters with the Ton-Ton Macoutes. Once they brought her one of their victims, horribly cut up, barely alive. She spent six hours sewing up the wounds in an attempt to save the man's life. Finally he was wheeled back to his room with attached tubes and IVs. He hadn't been there ten minutes before the Macoutes returned, jerked out all the tubes and dragged the man off. "And that," said my surgeon friend ruefully, "was the end of him."

The doctor then told me of another victim, a woman who had resisted the advances of one of the Macoutes. In a rage, the man responded by jabbing a knife up her vagina. Only emergency measures and hours of suturing managed to save the girl's life.

Many times as we returned from our French studies, we would find one of the Blue Boys sitting on the stairs with a machine gun across his lap. Often at night we heard them storm up the stairs, knock on someone's door and drag him off. Usually the victim was never seen again. The first few times this occurred our hearts raced with fear. After awhile, however, we learned to live with it. This was life in Haiti, and there was little we could do to change it. After a nightly raid by the Blue Boys, Valeene and I would pray and then drift back to sleep.

The hardest part of my being in Haiti was the separation from Sydney. Once a month I called her in the States. Haiti's phone system was infuriatingly antiquated, and it usually took several hours of waiting to get an available line. But any mother will understand why it was worth the wait. Those calls, hearing my daughter's happy voice, assuring me that she was O.K., telling me of latest developments in her life settled my heart. And our letters to one another revealed the continued peace we felt. Both of us, we knew, were just where we should be--in His will. But there were times when I ached to hold my daughter in my arms and just love her.

One night Valeene and I walked downtown so she could place a call to the States. After waiting one and a half hours she finally got through to her folks. It was the same old story of a poor connection. "I love you. Do you hear me?" Valeene kept shouting, but as often happened, though they could hear her, she could not hear them. Afterwards as we began walking back to the hotel, a small boy started following us. I guessed him to be one of the ubiquitous beggars that fill the streets of Haiti.

Finally he said, "My name is Jacque." I replied, "That's a nice name" still expecting him to ask us for money. Suddenly he took hold of our skirts and when we stopped he looked up and asked, "Do you love me?" "Yes, Jacque, we do love you," we responded. "We do truly love you."

We continued up the street, Jacque walking along with us when suddenly he just disappeared. We never saw Jacque again, although we returned to the same area several times. Afterwards I wondered if he could have been an angel sent by God to us that night when we were so aggravated, just to confirm within our hearts that we really did love the Haitians.

That year of language study in Port-au-Prince was one of the hardest in my life. I never learned to speak French well, but could read with good understanding which helped in so many ways. When I encountered the endless official papers or lists of medicines all written in French, I'd be so grateful for all the sweat and tears that I invested in the French language. Since virtually everyone in Haiti spoke Creole, however, and most preferred to speak it, I concentrated on this language and in time acquired enough fluency to carry on my medical work and even teach Bible classes.

Following language study Valeene and I returned to the OMS center in Vaudreuil, she to radio station 4VEH and I to the clinic. It soon became clear to me that I would have to find some convenient and efficient means of transportation to get me around Haiti. During these days there was a perpetual shortage of mission cars. Sometimes one had to sign up a week in advance to get a vehicle for either personal or ministry use. When I did manage to get one and prepared to leave the campus, a crowd of Haitian passengers would suddenly materialize all begging to be dropped off "along the way." So most of the time we just walked to wherever we needed to go.

Finally Tina Schwanke[3] and I ordered two Honda Trail 90 motorcycles from the U.S. It was a challenge learning to ride them since neither Tina nor I had ever been on a motorcycle before. Most of the missionaries held their breath as they watched us careening around the driveway, lurching and swerving from side to side. My naturally adventuresome spirit served me well. I loved it.

---

[3] Tina later married missionary evangelist Helmut Markeli. Today they serve with OMS in Indonesia.

And no mishaps, not even any scratches. I soon had the sturdy little vehicle completely under my control. Now we were able to come and go whenever we liked. I actually wore out three motorcycles during my time in Haiti.

Chapter Eleven

A Boy Named Samson

One day a little boy who had been terribly burned was brought to the clinic. His name was Samson. A younger sister, we learned, had pushed him against a pot of water boiling on a charcoal fire. The scalding water had splashed all over his chest and left arm. My heart wrenched within me as I dressed the burns. His tears flowed but he neither screamed nor cried out. Determined to be brave, he only grunted.

As the days and weeks passed I fell in love with that courageous, ever-smiling little boy. Then the day came when Samson opened his heart to Jesus. The whole clinic staff celebrated his new birth with candy and orange pop.

As time passed Samson's burns finally healed, but he didn't want to stop coming to see me. I asked if he would like to go to school, realizing his parents probably couldn't afford to send him. "Oh, yes," he replied, "but Poppa doesn't have any money." "Samson, I'll pay for your education and have two sets of school uniforms made for you," I said, "but there is one condition. You must earn this by being my errand boy and keeping my yard clean." He beamed in agreement. After that Samson became my shadow. Everywhere I went smiling Samson was usually there, and when I rode my motorcycle to make a house call Samson often rode on the back seat. If I held Child Evangelism classes out under a tree there was Samson to help lead the singing. If the kids started to leave Samson insisted that they come back, sit down and listen. (Although that seldom happens as all Haitian children love to sing and hear stories of Jesus.) If anyone wanted to be converted Samson would kneel down beside him. When I had visitors eating with me Samson would help my cook clean the rice, squeeze limes for the cold drink, and later clean pots and pans. Gradually as he grew older he helped with the cooking and became quite a little chef. I taught him a number of recipes including hushpuppies, which became his favorite food.

Samson really had a sense of humor. One day he brought me some delicious meat to taste. Thinking it was goat, the meat we usually ate, I took a generous portion. When I'd finished, he asked if I liked it. "Oh, I loved it," I raved, "just delicious." A few minutes later Samson started laughing and couldn't stop. "What's so funny?" I asked. "You know that wonderful meat you enjoyed so much?" he said. "Well, it wasn't goat, it was cat. You just ate a cat! It was a stray cat I caught in the mountains."

A week later when we had some visitors from the States, Samson caught and cooked another cat. I made him wait till the last night they were there before serving it along with the other meats. During the meal, Samson and I managed to pass the meat platter often, urging them to "eat hearty" since they'd be travling to Port-au-Prince to catch their plane the next day. Samson then asked me in Creole if he could tell them what they'd just eaten. "I think you'd better wait at least 30 minutes," I said. "We don't want them to get sick."

A half hour later Samson and I began to meow at each other. Puzzled, our guests finally asked what was going on. "We have a surprise for you," Samson said with an impish grin. "You just ate a cat!" He had to repeat the statement several times before the truth sank in. "Why you rascal!" the lady said as she jumped up and chased Samson out of the house and down the road. Samson enjoyed the joke so much that a few years later when Bob, Sidney and my grandchildren came to visit, he pulled the same trick on them.

Samson would often go with me to visit Frere Marcial, a dear Haitian man. The last time I visited him was just a few weeks before he died at the incredible age of 112. We had been prayer partners since the first year I arrived in Haiti. His enthusiasm for the Lord caught my attention during services in our church on the mission compound. If he saw someone sleeping during the service, he would walk over and shake the drowsiness right out of him and then return to his seat. Since this was a regular occurrence the pastor didn't even stop his sermon. If the people didn't sing with joy Frere Marcial would stop the song, reprimand everyone, and have them begin again. He shouted a spirited "Amen" to anything he felt came from God. Once in a while he called the preacher to stop while he asked the congregation if they were tongue-tied and couldn't say "Amen" too.

Frere Marcial's knowledge of the Bible was an inspiration to all of us missionaries. Unable to read or write he had committed long passages to memory. On occasion when I misquoted some Scripture he would immediately correct me. During my second term when I lived three miles away from the compound, he walked the distance just to pray with me. He did this with other missionaries as well, simply saying, "The Lord sent me."

Just before Christmas each year Samson and I would take a large basket of assorted foods as a gift to Frere Marcial. Of course we knew that he would share it with whomever happened by. One day I heard that his thatch roofed home was on fire. I arrived just as the walls were collapsing in flames. There, standing and looking on was Frere Marcial, wearing a skirt and blouse. He'd fallen asleep stark naked. A neighbor had to awaken him just in time to escape before the roof fell in. The neighbor then furnished him with a skirt and blouse. Soon after the fire some of our missionaries built him a new house with a tin roof.

The last time I saw Frere Marcial alive he said, "Isn't God good to us? He gave us His Son Jesus Christ. He gave us the Bible so that we could hear, listen and understand His Word. He even gave us the radio station 4VEH so we could hear about Jesus in our own language." As we left Marcial's home that day I turned to Samson and said, "Frere Marcial is truly a prophet, and once he is gone everyone will recognize that." Frere died just six weeks before his 113th birthday. He is buried in his own yard. I still miss that dear prayer partner.

Chapter Twelve

An Arena Of Life And Death

That little clinic in Vaudreuil was often an arena of considerable drama--the scene of both life and death. Looking back now I recall more than one episode that left us laughing, sometimes with delight and at other times from relief.

One morning a woman came running into my consulting room and rammed a baby's fanny into my face screaming, "Give him an enema, give him an enema!" I excused myself from the patient I had been working with and took the baby. He looked perfectly healthy to me, and after a few minutes the woman calmed down enough to tell me why the enema was needed. She had weaned the baby the week before. That afternoon she had laid down with the baby to take a nap. While she slept the baby had stolen milk from her breast. To her mind, since the baby had been weaned, that milk was poison, and it needed to be flushed out or the baby would die. It took some fast talking on my part to convince her that the milk had probably been the best food the baby had had all week. I'm sure that sneaky baby will get by in this world.

Yippee in my Soul!

Most Haitian mothers breast feed their babies. For them it is perfectly natural to pull out a breast and nurse the baby wherever they happen to be, whether in church, at home, talking to people, walking along the road or riding a donkey. Mealtime is mealtime.

One poor woman came to see me with a large breast abcess which was especially painful when she walked. My solution was to devise a sling for the breast. Most relieved she merrily went her way after receiving the medication. That sling idea caught on and soon I found other women with painful breasts also using the device.

I'll always remember a mother who brought her five-month old baby to the clinic. She claimed she had seen maggots appear in the abcess on the child's head. I probed and probed but could not find any maggots. Finally I asked my nurse assistant to check it out. She, too, was unsuccessful. But after the mother started crying and insisted she couldn't leave until we had seen them, suddenly two maggots stuck their heads up out of the hole. We were then able to remove them all, dress the wound and give medication. The mother left crying, but it was a happy cry this time. Her love and persistence had been rewarded. The next day she returned with the baby and brought gifts of eggs for both my assistant and me. We usually accepted such gifts even though we knew the tremendous sacrifice they represented. Our refusal would have hurt them more than the sacrifice.

We continued to treat for worms more than any

other ailment. One day we noted an unusual phenomenon. All the fecal lab results were showing the exact same (and not so common) parasite. Finally I questioned the lab technician who surmised there seemed to be a run of this parasite at this time of the year. Not satisfied I went out to one of our clinic workers and asked if he had noticed anything different going on. Were there a group of people in the waiting room who had come from the same area? Thirty minutes later he returned laughing. It seems that many of those sent to the latrine for a specimen couldn't produce. There was one enterprising young man who succeeding in doing so, and was selling small amounts of feces for $.05 each! Now who could get upset about that. It was actually one of the funniest things that ever happened at that clinic.

After some years an obstetrical nurse was finally assigned to the clinic. What a relief to have her assisting with the deliveries. One day she delivered twins, but one died shortly after birth. We sent word for the father to come, claim and bury the baby, as there was a law in Haiti that you must bury your dead within 24 hours.

A few hours later a man came to my consulting room. He said that he was an uncle and had permission from the nearby farmer to bury the baby in his garden. I told him to go to the red door (all the doors were painted different colors because most of the patients were illiterate) and the nurse would give him the baby. He went to the door, knocked and called for the nurse. When she didn't come he went in and found two babies, each wrapped in a receiving blanket. He took one and left. Ten minutes later the O.B. nurse came to my room asking where the live baby was. I told her about the man I had directed to her office. She said she had just returned to the office to find the live baby was gone. We looked at each other in horror.

I immediately sent the whole clinic staff out in every direction to search for the man. Five minutes later one of the staff shouted that he was at the gate entrance. I ran out to the gate as fast as I could. The man was standing there with a box in front of him. "What happened?" I said. "You got the wrong baby!" He answered, "It cried." He told us later that he had already dug the hole and was about to place the box with the baby in it when he heard a cry. We all had a good laugh and also praised the Lord for that baby's timely cry.

One night while lying in bed reading, someone knocked at the door and yelled, "Madame Bonnette, Madame Bonnette!" Hearing the urgent cry, I quickly grabbed a robe and ran to the front door. I learned that the woman was out on the lawn about to give birth to a baby. She'd tried to walk to the clinic, but had only gotten that far.

I always had one emergency kit in the house, and one at the clinic. I grabbed the kit and an umbrella, as it was starting to rain, and took off running. Sure enough that baby was making its entrance into the world and was not about to wait another minute. Right there in the yard, with the man holding the umbrella over us, I delivered the baby. That woman's front and my back got good and wet, but the baby was protected. I carried the infant under my robe as we walked the mother to the clinic where we had only one bed at that time, and soon the mother and baby were snug under the covers.

Before going back to bed I sent a bowl of warm soup to the woman. We kept her three days, and she enjoyed every minute of it. Had she delivered the baby at home she would have had to resume cooking and caring for the entire family immediately.

One patient I'll never forget is the 16-year-old boy who was brought to the clinic with a temperature of 106. He was actually dying. The mother who carried the boy kept saying "He wants to talk to you. Please, please talk to him."

"Would you like to talk to us about Jesus?" I asked. At this he broke into a big smile. With the help of a Haitian staff member I told him of Jesus after which he prayed a simple prayer asking Christ into his heart. His face became radiant as though illuminated by a heavenly light. I know now he was already entering the presence of his Lord. I asked the mother if she could send him to the city hospital. When she agreed we carried him to the clinic gate but before the vehicle arrived he had slipped away. The memory of that precious lad will always remain a special inspiration.

But after a long day at the clinic I sometimes found it was hard to be patient with Haitians who came to my door seeking help. One day after an especially grueling morning I trudged up to the house relishing the thought of food, rest, and no patients. Nurse Flo Boyer and I had just finished eating lunch when a woman knocked on the screen door. Irritated I remarked to Flo, "Watch me get rid of this one in a hurry." I went to the door and before the woman could say anything I blurted out, "The clinic's that way and I'll be there in a few minutes." In a soft voice she replied, "Madame Bonnette, there is nothing wrong with me. I just came to pray with you." I felt like a rat hunting for a hole. What a lesson in humility from the Lord. From that time on I never turned anyone away day or night for any reason.

Often to relieve the strain and escape the ceaseless demands of patients at the clinic or at my house I found a motorcycle ride the perfect antidote. One afternoon arriving home completely wrung out, I found Samson waiting for me.

"How about going for a ride?" I asked. "Min oui!" (but yes) was his happy response.

So with Samson seated on the back, I sped through the city of Cap Haitian, over the mountain and down to the ocean. When we arrived at the beach, I parked the bike and walked right into the water, uniform, shoes and all. "Ooh-la-la!" I let out a sigh like a contented cow. Samson's eyes widened and his mouth fell open. Then in an instant he joined me, clothes and all.

Other times I came home from the clinic hardly able to move or think. One more decision, I felt, and my brain would short-circuit. It always helped to burst out in song with "La joie de L'Eternal sera votre force" which means "The joy of the Lord is my strength." Or even let out with some crazy ditty like, "Mares eat oats and does eat oats and little lambs eat ivy." Maybe those were times when I actually had blown a fuse topside. Still the Lord always gave an extra measure of grace to face another day, fulfilling His promise that "As your days so shall your strength be."

Chapter Thirteen

February 6! February 6! February 6!

Yes, I must admit that as far back as I can remember reminding people of my birthday has been great fun. From the time I was five, every year beginning in December or January my parents, relatives, and friends heard me chant those magic words. Of course, there were a few hazardous moments like the time my mother threatened to use the switch if she heard February 6 mentioned one more time. When this happened I just marked in the special date on all the calendars in the house. One year the large calendar in the kitchen appeared with all the days of February blacked out except one--February 6th!

Years later my husband and daughter were forced to endure the same treatment. Somehow little February 6 reminder notes would be found in my daughter's lunch pail or tucked onto her bulletin board. My husband discovered reminders on his car windshield, desk top, or in his briefcase or sock drawer.

My friends received subtle hints such as "Do you

February 6! February 6! February 6!

have anything planned for February 6?" Or they'd receive phone calls which said, "This is a recording, February 6, February 6, February 6." So for years people have lovingly suffered, finding some consolation in the knowledge that once February 6 passed they had a 10-month reprieve before reminders started up again.

My Haiti missionary friends caught the brunt of it. One year, not wanting to take any chances, I gave myself a birthday party and invited all our missionaries plus my Haitian friends. There was lots of food, laughs, and gifts of chocolate. I wonder how they knew I liked Chocolate?! After that every year the missionaries gave me a party.

Other years I made and sent my friends throughout the world a ribbon bookmark inscribed with the words "MERRY CHRISTMAS AND REMEMBER FEBRUARY 6!" Another year I made clay Haitian huts with February 6 carved on the base and a cartoon of me yelling "February 6" across the ocean to friends in the U.S.

Learning that Ronald Reagan's birthday is also February 6, I sent a greeting to him in the White House along with a cartoon congratulating him that his birthday was on the same day as mine. He responded with a personal letter saying that it was a pleasure to know we celebrated the same birth date.

One year my reminders were so excessive that when February arrived, I thought it might be wise for me to head for the hills, literally. Instead I decided to call February 6 an illegal holiday and take the day off.

Yippee in my Soul!

My born-again birthday is March 14, 1959, the day Jesus Christ became my personal Savior. That's a birthday I like to celebrate every day--recalling the miracle of Jesus' birth in my soul. I wouldn't hesitate to shout it from the housetops or mountaintops.

Chapter Fourteen

Friends And Angels

During my years in Haiti, God gave me two special friends. One of them was Valeene Hayes, who was with me in Port-au-Prince for language study. The other was Archie Bell.

Valeene and I shared an apartment and spent a lot of time together. Yet our ministries were quite different. While my days were spent in the clinic, she was in charge of music at radio station 4VEH. Valeene is an accomplished pianist and a marvellous choir director. From the very beginning we understood and trusted each other.

At age seven Valeene had rheumatic fever, resulting in a serious heart condition. She was often carried around by her father during her growing-up years. She gradually improved and despite the doctor's strong reservations managed to get to the mission field. Yet if she became too exhausted, her heart would act up. One night after several tiring weeks, she went to bed with severe heart pains. The generator which provided our electricity on the compound was shut down each night at 10 o'clock due to a fuel shortage. That meant no lights. Keenly aware of my roommate's suffering, I was sitting by her bed in the dark praying. Suddenly I looked up to see several tiny angels busily working inside her chest. "Have I been asleep? Am I dreaming?" I wondered.

Valeene awakened shortly and said, "Margaret, I feel so much better." I placed my stethoscope to her chest and found that her heartbeat was normal. What a contrast to the erratic pounding I'd heard earlier. I told her about the angels I had seen. We both began to cry and thank the Lord for His mercy.

At other times when I was far away in the mountains I would suddenly be impressed that I should get to Valeene. I would arrive at her side just when needed. She, too, did the same for me. David had his Jonathan. I had my Valeene.

My other special friend was Archie Bell. She and her husband served as independent missionaries in the interior of Haiti. This amazing lady was another gift from the Lord. We know that when entering heaven we will be changed. Archie Bell will have to change less than anyone I know.

Several of my Christmas holidays were spent with the Bells at their home, about 35 miles from our mission station. Usually I rode my motorcycle there. Instead of celebrating with gifts for each other, we would have a large meal, inviting some of the Haitian pastors and their wives. Afterwards Archie and I would gather up candies, breads, and other Christmas goodies and walk back into the boonies. Soon children from the villages would start following us. When we had about 20 of them in our wake, we would stop and hold a little service with lots of singing and clapping of hands. We knew these kids would then take the Gospel song back to their homes where many of their parents were voodoo worshippers. In this way children have brought their entire families to the Lord. After the singing Archie and I would tell the kids about Jesus and give out the goodies. Then we would walk on and do the same with another group. I loved that way of celebrating Christmas.

On one of my visits to the Bell's home, I took the local bus. The next day while enjoying a cup of coffee I heard the shrill sound of wailing. I knew that meant that someone had died. When we ran out to the road to ask a passerby what had happened, we learned that the same bus which I had ridden the day before had gone over the side of the mountain, and many had been killed.

The wailing increased in volume as word of the tragedy spread. In less than 30 minutes, the wailing became a roar. It reminded me a little of what hell must be like.

Chapter Fifteen

"*You Must Come To Ti Bois*"

Though I found the work in the clinic in Vaudreuil tremendously satisfying, what I loved best were the treks into remote mountain areas for outstation clinics. Since our staff usually included two nurses (except when one was on furlough), it was often possible for one of us to travel to distant churches to hold clinics while the other kept things going at the compound.

For these forays into the boonies I would usually take a Haitian assistant with me and sometimes Samson as well. Our baggage consisted of a box full of medicines, some food for lunches along the way, and a sack of penny toys and chewing gum for the kids. To reach our destination we travelled by motorcycle, bus, jeep or Landrover as far as possible. When the roads deteriorated, often becoming narrow footpaths, we would have to resort to horse, donkey or foot. When I returned from these outstation clinics I was always saddle sore and and my feet ached as well.

"You Must Come To Ti Bois"

I began to dream of some day holding an out-station clinic at Ti Bois, a small village on top of a mountain in one of Haiti's most wretchedly impoverished areas, 100 miles from Cap Haitien. The founder and pastor of the church there was Julienne Joseph, a kindly gentleman, small in stature but mighty in the eyes of the Lord. In the four years he'd been at Ti Bois, marvelous things had taken place, beautiful evidence of the life-changing power of the gospel. Without even the most rudimentary medical services available, however, life for the poor, mountain peasants was an endless toll of physical suffering. "Madame Bonnette," Pastor Julienne pled, "you must come and help my people. They suffer so much. If you'll come and hold a clinic we can share the good news with all who come. There are so many yet to be reached for Jesus."

Another person who shared our burden for Ti Bois was Laurette, a beautiful Bible school student. A simple village girl, she had originally worked in the home of our missionaries, Hudson and Lucy Hess, serving as a kitchen helper. Impressed by her warm, outgoing personality and zealous witness, they had sent Laurette to our Emmaus Vocational Bible School. She was an outstanding student. She loved child evangelism and had a wonderful way with children. Laurette and I often went to churches to hold child evangelism classes. Recently she had conducted a nine-day vacation Bible school at Ti Bois, and had returned with a deep burden for the desperate physical and spiritual needs of the people there. She reported that almost everyone in the area was afflicted with chic disease, a disease which is caused by tiny fleas burrowing under

Yippee in my Soul!

the skin. This produces blister-like eruptions, principally on the feet. These blisters often become infected resulting in painful, foul-smelling sores, which can leave the victim permanently lame. "Madame Bonnette," she said, "if you hold a clinic at Ti Bois, please let me go along as your assistant. God has given me a great burden for the people there."

Day by day the desire to go to Ti Bois increased until I became convinced that God was drawing me to that forlorn village. Several days passed and the Lord continued to speak, the still small voice becoming more and more insistent. Excitement began to build up within me. I was certain this was God's time for us to go for a visit. Laurette and I began to pray together for God's direction in every area.

Further confirmation came when I met with our field superintendent, Mardy Picazo, asking permission to take a few days off for the trip. He responded with enthusiasm and gave his blessing to the undertaking. Our team would consist of a Haitian nurse, Laurette and I. Laurette told me that she had been unable to sleep at night just thinking of the people in Ti Bois. "We want you to go with us," I told her, "and be sure to take your child evangelism material with you."

We set the date for our departure and began organizing and preparing our provisions. Medical supplies were packed in one pillow case, food and clothing in another, with cans of boiled water in a third.

We would leave on Monday, the day that the vacationing nurse returned. We worked in the clinic until 4:00 p.m., and by 8:00 p.m. we were on a bus heading south towards Hostin, a small village about 90 miles away. After a full day at the clinic we were already weary when we began the torturous, bone-jarring seven-hour bus ride. All of us were crowded into the narrow 40-inch-long seats, three to a seat. Every time I sought a new position for my feet, two chickens squawked in protest. At 3:30 a.m. the bus jostled to a stop directly in front of Pastor Jeancius Seide's house. He had been expecting us, and gave us a gracious welcome and a good bed where exhausted we collapsed for a few hours' sleep.

After a quick breakfast we were ready for the long climb to Ti Bois. The pastor furnished us with two horses. One, we took turns riding, and the second carried our supplies.

Riding a horse up Haiti's narrow mountain trails is a skill that takes some time to acquire. I had been on a horse only once before coming to the field. I had a lot to learn. Haitian horses are small animals and are equipped with neither bits nor stirrups. The clumsy wooden saddle is an ingenious instrument of torture. Though I padded it as best I could with pillow or folded blanket I inevitably came to the end of the ride truly saddle sore. What usually hurt worse were my feet, since much of the journey was always made by foot. This was long before the age of Nike, Puma, and Air Jordans, and a few trips over Haitian trails would leave my sneakers limp and tattered. Going down the steep inclines was always the worst. Every step my toes doubled up painfully in my shoes. My feet would ache for days.

The first part of our journey from Hostin to Ti Bois was enjoyable. The trail led us across a pleasant stretch of plain that took us to the foot of a towering mountain the summit of which was our destination. The trail became steeper and steeper, part of it a narrow shelf carved into the side of a cliff with a precipitous gorge yawning down below us. Before long we found ourselves "bouki net" as the Haitians would say--completely exhausted. The trail was getting steeper and more rocky. The sun was beating down upon us, causing my heart to pound and my head to throb. I felt I was nearing the point of complete physical exhaustion. "Lord," I prayed, "this is tough. You've got to give me Your strength to keep me going."

Chapter Sixteen

A Desolate Scarred Mountain

After three and a half hours we arrived at the home of Pastor Julienne in the village of Ti Bois. I say village, but even the word village is too grandiose, for Ti Bois, I discovered, is nothing more than a cluster of shabby huts on the top of a desolate, scarred mountain. In this area, as throughout much of Haiti, virtually all the trees have been cut down. The result is terrible erosion and a dearth of top soil. What soil there is looks like fine white dust. It is as though the entire area had been sprayed with talcum powder. Even the children were white at Ti Bois. Goats and corn are about the only things raised in this area. It is pitiful to watch these peasants trying to plant their crops. They drive machetes down into what worn-out soil they can find between the ubiquitous rocks, drop two or three grains of corn in the hole and step on it. Of course, there is never any rest for the fields, and no one can afford fertilizer. The result is a diet that is pitifully inadequate and an infant mortality rate that is one of the highest in the world.

After arriving, we excused ourselves and retired to

the church, stretching out on the benches for a short rest before setting up a makeshift clinic. Soon one of the nurses was aroused by a familiar itching behind her right shoulder. It didn't take her long to discover the culprits-- two bedbugs which had taken refuge in a crack in the bench. They were quickly exterminated with the help of a trusty knife. Altogether during the rest period six bedbugs were killed, each gorged with her blood. Praise the Lord, Laurette and I were able to sleep in spite of the battle going on between our nurse and the tiny invaders.

Soon our first patients began arriving and it was time to set up the clinic. The water supply was too limited for bathing, but an adequate amount was available for drinking. Hot and sticky, we commenced unpacking and arranging the medical supplies. We felt like special God-assigned pioneers, realizing that this was the very first clinic ever held in the area. At 12:00 o'clock the church doors were opened and in minutes the benches were filled. Some of the patients, however, lingered outside and appeared hesitant to come in. They confided to Laurette that since they were not yet Christians they were afraid to enter the church. She assured them they were welcome and helped them find seats inside. We began singing a few songs and this was followed by a time of prayer and then a Bible story by Laurette.

Although our primary reason for coming to Ti Bois had been to treat those afflicted with chic disease, we discovered that many of the victims were too ashamed to be seen and treated in such a clinic. We sent out word for them to come assuring them we would gladly treat them.   The cruel, remorseless existence of people there was reflected in the patients who came to our little clinic. Many wore clothing so ragged that one wondered how it held together.   Small children, however, had no such problem. They wore nothing at all.

In Ti Bois even the most basic necessities of life were difficult to obtain.   The nearest water was a small spring halfway down the mountain.   It took the women a full hour to make the trip.   I watched with a heavy heart these small, frail women trudging up the mountain with the heavy containers on their heads.   I paid six women ten cents apiece to fetch the water we needed.

Although this first day we were not treating the chic disease patients as we had expected, we were continually amazed to discover that the medicines we had brought were exactly what was needed for the patients who came.   Approximately 50 were treated that first afternoon, many suffering from ulcerated sores.

With the sun beating down mercilessly, we prayed for rain and the rain came in the late afternoon and evening.   The Haitians laughed at us as we went outside and stood in the blessed, refreshing downpour.   Most Haitians fear rain because they chill and catch colds easily. Do you suppose there is a Haitian expression about the crazy Americans who do not have enough sense to come in out of the rain?

Knowing it would take some time to cook supper over a wood fire we closed the clinic at 5:00 p.m.   Bean soup never tasted better. Of course, the thick aromatic Haitian coffee is always worth waiting for.

As a missionary, one must accept people as they are. This means putting up with manners that in another setting would be unforgivably rude. In a Haitian village privacy is a luxury and virtually unknown. People are always present and watching your every move. Some of these Haitians had probably never seen a white woman before. I had to learn to accept their staring and gaping as a perfectly natural behavior. In their place I realized I would have done the very same thing.

Following supper we enjoyed a precious time of fellowship with the pastor and his family. We felt as though God was putting His loving seal of approval on the entire day as Brother Julienne humbly bowed his head, clasped his hands and thanked God for bringing us to Ti Bois.

No one had to urge us to go to bed that night; however, there was a slight delay since our sleeping accommodations were to be in the church on those same bedbug-ridden benches we had rested on that afternoon. We took pains to carefully spray insect repellent on the benches, sheets and ourselves. Gratefully the cool night air and the absence of bedbugs allowed us a good, refreshing night's sleep.

We awakened the next morning to the sound of giggles and childish chatter. I chuckled to watch a tangle of little children, their heads thrust into the doorway,

(L. to R.) Margaret, sister Helen and cousins. Broken Bow, OK, 1927.

Age 17. Her senior year in high school, 1940.

Margaret and Virgil, shortly after their wedding, 1943.

Hunting pheasant near Niagara Falls, NY.

(L. to R.) Sisters Helen and Nona, Margaret and mother.

Virgil, Sidney and Margaret, Niagara Falls, NY, 1957.

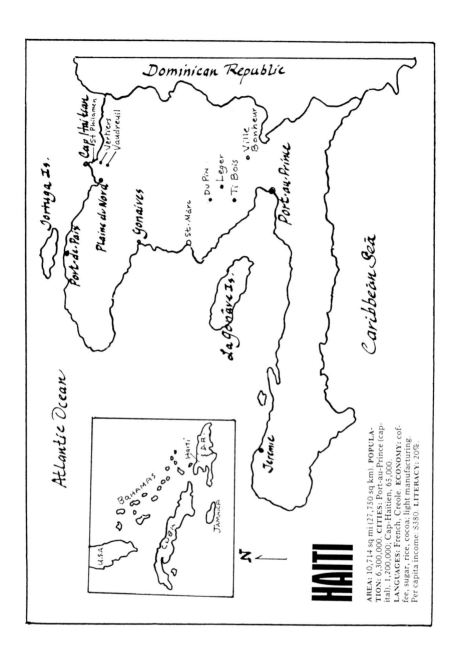

Dominican Republic

Atlantic Ocean

Tortuga Is.

Cap Haitian
St Philamen
Verters
Vaudreuil

Ville
Bonheur

Port-de-Paix

Plaine du Nord

Gonaïves

Du Pin
Leger
Ti Bois

Port-au-Prince

St. Marc

La Gonâve Is.

Caribbean Sea

Jeremie

BAHAMAS

HAITI
D.R.

CUBA

JAMAICA

U.S.A.

N

HAITI

AREA: 10,714 sq mi (27,750 sq km). **POPULA-TION:** 6,300,000. **CITIES:** Port-au-Prince (capital), 1,200,000; Cap-Haitien, 65,000. **LANGUAGES:** French, Creole. **ECONOMY:** coffee, sugar, rice, cocoa; light manufacturing. Per capita income: $380. **LITERACY:** 20%.

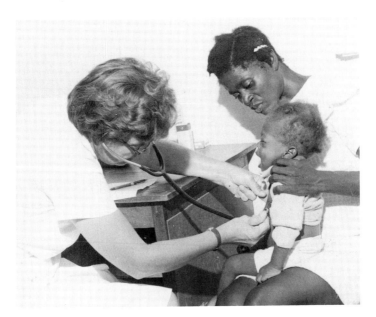

Vaudreuil clinic. Time for a "piki."

Nurses at Vaudreuil clinic. (L. to R.) Dorothy Irvine, Virginia Bailey, Margaret, Esther Close, Flo Boyer, Grandma B (Flo's mother).

"Motorcycle Missionary"

My room with prayer list on ceiling.

Children at Cowman School celebrating my birthday, Feb. 6.

Samson, showing scars from burns.

In Port-au-Prince for French language study. (L. to R.) Margaret, Douliane Sandez, Valeene Hayes.

With Haitian saddle.

My mountain climbing sneakers with cut-out toes.

Enroute to outstation clinics.

My favorite mount.

"This may hurt a little."

Outstation clinic.

All packed and ready to go.

Treating the sick in a mountain village.

Bob and Sidney's wedding, Dec. 20, 1969, in Estes Chapel, Wilmore, KY.

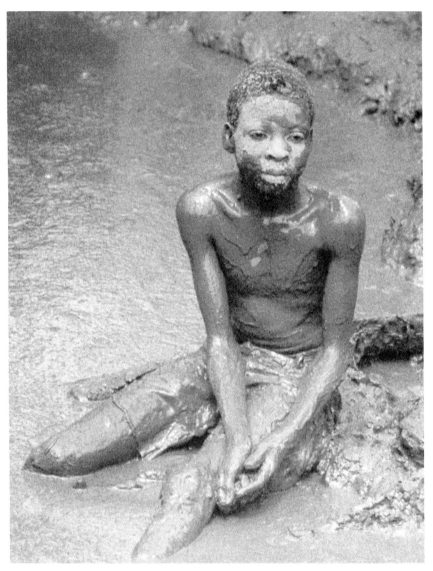

Voodoo worshipper in pool of St. Jacques, Plaine Du Nord.

With my Isuzu. Helping MFMers build my house at Leger.

My new home.

My "three musketeers."

The boys with my grandchildren, Philip, Audrey and Allison.

Samson at Radio 4VEH.

Samson with wife, Edoise, and baby, Fernando.

"Motorcycle Missionary" on furlough.

At home at Bradenton Missionary Village, Bradenton, FL.

working up courage to dart into the church. There were no locks so this wasn't difficult. When one of them did come in, Pastor Julienne and Laurette would good-naturedly chase them out, giggles and all.

By the time the service began at 7:30 a.m. the church was packed. Any lingering sleepiness was quickly disbursed by the joyous sound of Tiboisians singing at the top of their voices and clapping heartily to the glory of the Lord. We joined in and loved every minute of it.

None of the patients wanted to leave without the mandatory "piki" (injection) which they were convinced could heal anything from a headache to an infected foot. The injection room was just a sheet draped next to the door allowing a modicum of privacy while a bottom was bared for the insertion of the needle. Many of our patients came with leg ulcers so deep that the bone was visible. Often the shocking condition of these ulcers was the result of a popular Haitian treatment which called for placing rotten banana leaves inside the wound. Although this simply increased the infection, retarding the healing process, they continued to practice the same old custom. Simple instruction in basic health and sanitation was what was so desperately needed here.

Several of those who came had horribly diseased scalps, covered by thick matted hair which had never been cut. The only solution was to shave the entire head. We were glad we'd packed a few new razor blades in our supplies, although at the time we had not known why. Praise the Lord! He had guided us even in the little things.

Chapter Seventeen

"You Must Come Back"

One of the joys of the morning came when one of our Christian patients, a member of the church, presented us with a love gift--six ears of corn. Knowing how hard it is to wrest a crop from those barren hillsides, that simple offering was, in our eyes, as precious as gold. But this was typical of the way Haitians expressed their appreciation for any kindness shown them.

Busy with all of the morning's activities noon came quickly. Further treatment was suspended so we could pack to leave. From the start of the clinic everyone had been very orderly, but now as the patients saw us preparing for departure, they began to panic, pushing, crowding, calling pitifully for our attention. This made our work more difficult, but I sympathized with their feelings. They realized that this could very well be the last opportunity for them to receive medical aid.

Soon it was time to leave. Everyone gathered outside the church to bid us farewell. I looked into the faces of these simple folk, many of them smiling with the beautiful radiance that comes from life in Jesus Christ. I thought how the vision of one man, dear Pastor Julienne, had turned them from darkness to light and from the power of Satan unto God.

I was loading one last item on the pack horse when I suddenly felt a heavy foot on top of my own. It was the horse's. Unable to move I lost my balance and sprawled unceremoniously backward onto the ground. But praise the Lord, the only injury was to my pride! Finally we gathered in a circle. Pastor Julienne prayed for journeying mercies and gave thanks for all that had been accomplished during the past two days. A chorus of voices now begged us to return. "Come back, Madame Bonnette," they pleaded, "we need you; don't forget us. You must come back to Ti Bois soon."

At the beginning of our descent a few strangely decorated houses caught my attention. Upon questioning some of those who lived nearby we learned that the previous owners of these houses had been devil worshippers. The new owners, Christians, had repainted the outside walls, not using ordinary paint, but rather ochre of different colors. Then, on the newly painted walls, squares were drawn with crude, but colorful pictures inside depicting aspects of their daily lives. They called this "baptizing" their homes.

Remembering the steep ascent to Ti Bois we felt some apprehension realizing that these trails were even harder to negotiate when going down. We were somewhat relieved, however, to discover that the pastor had assigned us three guides. These small boys went ahead leading the horses and directing whatever traffic approached us on the narrow path. This was one time we were thankful to be using the British traffic system. Hugging and often scrapping the mountain on the left was better than being on the right where we could look straight down hundreds of feet. By late afternoon we reached the foot of the mountain, tired and out of breath.

A short time later we arrived at Pastor Jean's home where we had rested that night before the ascent to Ti Bois. He already had a few patients waiting. Although exhausted we reopened the pillow case of medicines and within a short time a small clinic was being held in the backyard.

One family had arrived the night before carrying their eight-year-old son. They had heard that a white nurse was in the vicinity. The child was pitifully malnourished, his body swollen, his hair reddish, on his face the typical apathetic expression. After treating him with what medicine we had, we explained to the parents the importance of providing him with milk, realizing at the same time that on their meager income this was probably an impossibility and without proper food he would die. I knew that there were literally thousands of children in this area in the very same condition as this little boy.

That night the pastor and his wife graciously gave up their bedroom for us, and the bed was a welcome sight indeed. Soon, however, I found myself struggling to accept with grace one of those infuriating aspects of foreign culture which often leave us foreigners so upset. The one window which could have provided desperately needed ventilation was closed. The air was muggy, stifling, and the room almost like an oven. This was typical. Most Haitians close their rooms tight as a drum at night. More than a superstitious fear of the unhealthy night air, I realized that this was also done for our protection, from nocturnal visitors in the form of large, hungry rats. Situations like this tend to make one reflect on the blessing of simple aspects of western civilization and things like screened windows.

We awakened the next morning to the familiar cacophony of a Haitian village greeting the day with the shrill cry of the rooster along with the playful banter of small children. Already there were patients at the door waiting to be attended. When we had treated the last of them it was time for breakfast. The graciousness of Pastor Jean and his wife was touching. Their love was shown to us in so many little ways. Along with a nourishing breakfast we were served the wonderful Haitian coffee, not just one pot but two--one with sugar and one without. I realized that by Haitian standards this represented the epitome of hospitality.

Not wishing to miss the first bus to Cap Haitien we decided to wait at the side of the road until it arrived. While sitting there the pastor told me of a decision he had made during the night. "Madame Bonnette," he said, "do you remember that malnourished child that was brought to the clinic yesterday? Well, we just cannot let him die and decided to take him to a hospital in Port-au-Prince."

Yippee in my Soul!

I was moved again by this man's loving concern for his people, for their physical needs as well as their spiritual. I knew, too, that expenses for this trip would come out of his own pocket at tremendous personal sacrifice. But now there was hope for the child's recovery.

Just prior to the arrival of the bus we were surprised to see Pastor Julienne from Ti Bois approaching us. He greeted us with a broad smile, and we talked together of the joys of the past two days. He said that people from the distant mountains were still arriving in Ti Bois. They had heard of the clinic and had come seeking medical treatment only to be disappointed in finding us gone. Our joys were mingled with feelings of helplessness and the sadness of so many needs unmet.

We boarded the bus for the return trip to the OMS center in Vaudreuil reliving the busy, hectic, happy hours of ministry in Ti Bois, thinking of the many whose lives had yet to be touched by the Gospel and of the wide open door to reach them. This was a picture all too common. Multitudes so needy, so eager, and yet unreached. And always the endless procession of patients pleading for compassion and ease from their daily burden of pain.

This trip to Ti Bois had been God's plan carried out. We had walked literally in obedience to His leading. Now we had to leave the rest of the results in His hands.

Chapter Eighteen

A Door Open Wide

One summer afternoon during my third term in Haiti, a knock at my door set in motion an amazing chain of events. My visitor was Monsieur Jean Methelus, a member of our Plaine du Nord church and the owner of an outdoor bakery about one mile from our mission compound. The two of us made our way to the side of the house, placing our chairs beneath the old mango tree.

First, as is the Haitian custom, there was the inevitable exchange of pleasantries and inquiries concerning one's health and family. Then Monsieur Methelus paused and cleared his throat. I knew this meant he was about to reveal the reason for his visit. "Madame Bonnette," he began, "last night the Lord appeared to me in a vision. There were three of us--you, Pastor Mark, and myself. The Lord told us to go to the St. Philomen residential area just outside the gate to the city of Cap Haitien. When we entered that area I saw a large door opening wide before us, and finally the Lord said to us 'Go quickly, you must go quickly.'"

Yippee in my Soul!

I looked into the earnest face of my friend. Haitians with their background of voodoo and superstitions have lively imaginations, but there was something so genuine, so sincere in Jean's recital of his experience that I felt a tingle of excitement run up my spine as he spoke. "Brother Methelus," I said, "I'll pray about this. If this vision is really of the Lord I want the Holy Spirit to confirm it in my own heart, and meanwhile, I think it would be good if you'd talk to Pastor Mark. I'll give you my answer soon."

During the next few days I found my thoughts continually occupied with Pastor Methelus and his amazing vision. As I thought and prayed it came to me with growing conviction that this revelation to a simple Haitian lay-pastor was indeed of the Lord.

Three days later, Pastor Mark came to see me. He had talked with Brother Methelus. Both of us agreed that we must respond in obedience to the Lord's clear direction even if it meant changing our busy schedules. We consented to meet with Jean the following week. Meanwhile, we would continue to pray. Three days later the three of us joined by Brother Ennis, a singing evangelist, met at the pastor's home. First, Jean repeated the account of his vision. After a time of prayer we mounted our motorcycles and rode to the area of the city identified in the vision. This was a fairly new residential section and none of us had ever been there. We parked our cycles and began to walk from street to street to see what would happen. People greeted us warmly wherever we went.

Finally, after several hours, we arrived at the top of the hill which marks the end of the development. There were only two or three houses in this area. Just outside the first, sat an old woman selling whiskey and bread. Standing near her was a middle-aged woman and several men. While I witnessed to the ladies the other members of our team spoke to the men urging them to give their lives to Christ. All listened attentively, but no decisions were made that day. Time came to leave and we told everyone that we would return in one week.

The four of us went back to Pastor Mark's house, praising God. Excitement was building. We sensed that the Holy Spirit had something special in store for us. After prayer we dispersed and agreed to meet at the same place the following week.

Thursday arrived and we again were on our motorcycles enroute to the site of Jean Methelus' vision. This time we divided into two teams. Methelus with his friend, Brother Ennis, the singing evangelist, and Pastor Mark with me. Each team would cover a specified area of the neighborhood, and then we'd meet at 5:00 p.m. at our rendezvous point.

I rode my motorcycle to the top of the hill, the area where the pastor and I had agreed to begin our visitation. Soon I met the two women I had spoken to on the previous visit. This time the middle-aged lady had her sixteen-year-old son with her. She smiled broadly when she saw me coming. "Madame," she said earnestly, "we want to be converted." My jaws must have dropped open

Yippee in my Soul!

at this amazing greeting. "Right now?" I asked incredulously. "Yes," they replied, "right now. We want to be converted right now." I told them that the pastor was walking up the hill and would be there in a few minutes. In the meantime, I suggested we sit down on a pile of rocks while I read some verses from the Bible.

In a few minutes Pastor Mark arrived and was surprised to find two souls already entering the Kingdom of God. All of us knelt with our heads resting on that pile of rocks as the mother and son asked Jesus to come into their hearts. "While we were praying," the mother explained a little later, "I felt as if my heart were growing larger and larger. My heart became so big I felt as though my whole body would explode."

Meanwhile, the other team was also discovering that the Holy Spirit had prepared hearts for our coming. Two people accepted the Lord shortly after they arrived. Pastor Mark and I continued on to another house. We talked to an old man who listened quietly, but said he was not ready to make a decision. Approaching the next house we heard raucous music issuing from a radio. Through the windows we could see two teenage girls, their bodies gyrating in a frenzied dance. The pastor asked if they could come outside, so we could talk to them. They nodded agreement, turned off the radio, and brought chairs outside for all of us. Haitians are very gracious to visitors. If they do not have enough chairs, they will borrow some from a neighbor. Sitting there in the courtyard the pastor and I explained the four spiritual laws to the girls, and within thirty minutes both of them had received Christ. By this time it was getting quite late so we decided to leave the area and return the following week. As we mounted our motorcycles and headed back, our hearts were overflowing with praise. Eight had entered God's Kingdom that day. The open door that Brother Methelus had seen in his vision had become a reality. All God had needed was a few willing servants to walk through that door. Week after week the four of us continued to meet, pray, and then return to the St. Philomen area. Every time, without exception, there were prepared hearts just waiting, as it were, for our coming, already willing to accept the Lord as their Savior.

After one month we put up an arbor church consisting of poles with bamboo thatching for a roof--not much to look at, but a place where we could meet with new babes in Christ, a living, thriving part of the body of Jesus Christ.

By the middle of July there were 37 Christians in St. Philomen. It was now time to look for a building to use as a church. Then amazingly, even before we had formerly started our search, a man offered us a new cinder block building perfect for our needs. The rent was $100 a year. Within a week the Lord gave us that exact amount.

We started having Sunday school and church services. Bible studies were held two or three nights a week. Later a grade school was begun for the believers' children. Every week it seemed the door was being pushed open a little wider. By the following year the rented building had become too small for the ever-growing congregation. A team of Men For Missions laymen came to the field and helped the believers erect a beautiful new sanctuary. Since that time the St. Philomen church has continued to grow and thrive, a beautiful monument to a simple Haitian man's obedience to the revelation of God. When I left Haiti God was still bringing people in through that open door.

Chapter Nineteen

"Awful Things Happen There"

Because life in Haiti is so hard, holidays and festivals are looked forward to with great anticipation as an opportunity to, for a moment, forget poverty and misery, finding a brief escape from the drab, miserable existence. Mardi Gras in Haiti, as in New Orleans, is a Catholic carnival which provides sanction for unbridled lust and indulgence of the most carnal of human appetites. "Rara" is a wild, often drunken parade, usually lasting for three days--Good Friday through Sunday. We tried to avoid getting caught in these melees. The celebrants are often completely drunk on clarin, the cheap local booze. Abandoning all inhibitions they perform licentious dances, working themselves into a frenzy, eventually losing all control. That's when anything can happen and often does.

One year Sue Martin, another missionary nurse, and I were invited to our friends, the Bells, for the weekend. When we planned the trip we had not realized that we would be heading home during the days of Rara. Sunday afternoon we began the long journey back to

Yippee in my Soul!

Vaudreuil. Soon, however, we began to meet groups of people painted with wild colors, some half-naked with only loin clothes over their heavily greased bodies. Others were dressed in bizarre costumes. Beeping our horns we managed to thread our way through two groups. When we saw a much larger contingent coming our direction, I began to sense a kind of fear I had never felt before. As we advanced I beeped my horn but could see that the people, agitated and quite clearly under the influence of liquor, were reluctant to yield. They finally allowed us an opening, but I could see livid hatred on their faces. As we slowly made our way through the jostling crowd, Sue's motorcycle suddenly died. This had never happened before. "Sue," I said, "you keep trying to get it started and I'll smile and pray." She tried and tried but it just would not start.

Then the group began to move menancingly towards us, but they could only get so close. It was clear that they intended to harm us in some way, but it was as though they encountered an invisible barrier. They could not seem to touch us. Finally the bike started, and we managed to drive on through. A few blocks away and around a bend in the road we stopped, got off our motorcycles, and knelt beside the road to thank the Lord for His protection. Our guardian angels probably said to themselves, "What mess will they get into next?"

July is the great festival month in Haiti. On the 16th, tens of thousands of pilgrims congregate at Ville Bonheur, sixty miles east of Port-au-Prince for the festival of St. Jean Baptiste. In a shameless mixture of

94

"*Awful Things Happen There*"

Catholicism and voodoo, Haitians gather at the beautiful waterfall Saut d'Eau to worship Vyejmirak-Mary, the virgin of miracles, reputed to have appeared in that area to a 19th century peasant and the serpent god Danbala Wedo. He and his wife, Aida, are believed to inhabit the beautiful waterfalls. Worshippers gather under the cascading falls and throw themselves with abandon into the pools, on occasion going into seizures--a sign that the spirit of Danbala has possessed them.[4]

On the 25th of July an even larger festival is held in the village of Plaine du Nord, located just five miles from the OMS center at Vaudreuil. Here also, in a crude admixture of voodoo and Christian tradition, the festival honors St. Jacque Majeur (St. James the Greater) along with Ogun Ferraille, an African god of war. Since early lithographs depict St. James on horseback brandishing a sword, he is viewed as the most warlike of the saints and a natural companion for Ogun Ferraille.

Whereas the festival of Vyejmirak is marked by natural beauty and the cleansing waters, the ceremonies of Plaine du Nord are foul and loathsome by contrast. Celebrants wade into the Troujacque, the St. James basin, a huge rectangular slough of mud believed to possess healing properties. Again they invoke the names of voodoo gods, singing and dancing themselves into a wild frenzy. When possessed by the spirits women quiver and writhe in the slime. Additional merit is obtained by

---

[4] For more on voodoo in Haiti, see appendix.

casting into the mud offerings of coins and food, usually rice, beans, rum and wine. This is a bonanza for village boys who scamper through the mud retrieving the coins.

Since the ferocious gods of war will be satisfied with nothing short of blood, Haitians slash their bodies allowing the blood to drip into the mud. The climax of the festival comes when sacrificial animals--goats and oxen--are led into the mud and hacked to death. The blood is caught in calabash gourds and drunk.

"Never go near Plaine du Nord during the St. Jacques' festival," I was sternly warned by my fellow missionaries, "awful things happen there! It is not safe!" But I must admit one year my curiosity got the better of me and I disobeyed that rule, a foolish thing to do. On the appointed day I rode my motorcycle to the outskirts of the village and parked near a Haitian friend's house. Then spotting two army soldiers that I had treated in the clinic I asked them to accompany me to the pool.

As we approached I could see thousands of people milling around, many drunk from the effects of cheap liquor. Slowly we plowed our way through. What a horrible sight! People were wading around in that filthy muddy pool, some with no clothes on. I shielded my camera as best I could and clipped off about eight pictures. The soldiers hurried me away back to my motocycle. I sent that roll of film to the States to be developed. All the prints were perfect except for the eight I had taken at the pool. Actually I thank God for I wanted no reminder of such devil worship.

"Awful Things Happen There"

The debauchery associated with the festival at the pool of St. Jacques in Plaine du Nord is a source of embarrassment to sensitive Haitians and particularly the growing number of evangelicals in the north. One of them, Pastor Tony Paul, determined to do something about it. Tony pastors the largest evangelical church in Plain du Nord, one which has planted 13 daughter churches. A graduate of OMS Emmaus Vocational Bible School, he is a big, ebulent man who oozes joy and good will and believes God actually answers the prayers of His people. Tony was the first Christian in a voodoo-worshipping home and was instrumental in leading his whole family to Christ. "The Devil has had Plaine du Nord long enough," he announced. "It's time for the Christians to let him know who has the real power."

Tony and other pastors in the area organized a parade for July 21, 1988--a time when Haiti was in more than unusual turmoil following the toppling of Baby Doc. They invited Christians in the area to meet at Tony's church in the morning to begin a nine-mile march to Cap Haitian. OMS supported the effort with enthusiasm, announcing it daily over radio 4VEH.

On the appointed morning nearly 500 showed up at Tony's church and the procession was begun. Uniformed members of the church's Boys Brigade (a kind of Christian Boys Scouts) led the way, assuring that the parade was orderly and would not impede or block traffic. At points along the way more Christians joined the parade. By the time they had reached the OMS center at Vaudreuil, four miles from Plaine du Nord, numbers had swelled to more than a thousand.

It is a moving thing to see a thousand, smiling Haitians singing praises to God at the top of their lungs. And how Haitians love to sing! Some carried banners; hundreds waved Bibles and song books. At intervals along the way, Tony would blow his whistle calling a brief halt for an impromptu street meeting. Fiery exhortations were followed by earnest prayers consecrating Haiti to the Lord Jesus Christ and defying the demonic powers of voodoo.

When the throng reached the outskirts of Cap Haitian, they numbered several thousand and nearly all of the city lined the streets to see this unprecedented phenomenon. Even newsmen and representatives of local radio stations turned out to observe and report. Coming to the large Y-shaped open area near the center of town, the procession stopped and assembled. Fervent singing was followed by exhortation. Then Tony Paul blew his whistle, a signal to let out with the triumphant cry, "Bene sois L'eternal!" (Blessed be the Lord!) The shout was repeated again and again with increasing fervor.

Then a most remarkable thing occurred. The people looked up to see a rainbow in the sky, but not a typical arching rainbow such as appears after a storm. This one formed a radiant full circle of color around the sun. People stood in open-mouthed wonder. Valeene Hayes, who was working at the 4VEH studio at the time, was called outside by a Haitian colleague to witness the amazing spectacle.

Newsmen, wide-eyed with wonder, approached Tony Paul. "What does it mean?" they demanded. "We have never seen a rainbow like it before." "Well," replied the inspired pastor, "when God put the first rainbow in the heavens, it was a covenant that He would show mercy to man and never again destroy the earth with water. Clearly this rainbow is God's covenant with Haiti--as a sign of His mercy. He will not destroy Haiti but bless it with the Gospel."

Since then, every year on July 21, Christians gather for the great parade which has now become a Christian tradition in the north. This amazing, united evangelical response has given birth to a prayer meeting that draws thousands of believers to the large Edith Robinson Auditorium in Cap Haitian on Saturdays. Originally held once a month, Christians were soon insisting that they must meet on a weekly basis. And so the church grows and God blesses.

Chapter Twenty

A House In Vertierres

Following my second furlough I returned to Haiti to begin my 13th year. As much as I had enjoyed my work in the clinic I found my heart increasingly drawn to the multitudes of Haitians in remote backwater villages, far from towns, living in misery and dying prematurely without ever receiving the medical help they so desperately needed. I asked to be assigned full time to an outstation ministry. My request was granted and during furlough I had raised funds for a jeep to facilitate trips over rough, all but impassable roads, into the interior. With the arrival of Dr. Bourke from New Zealand and two short-term RNs, I knew that the clinic was in capable hands.

Compound living, though much maligned by missiologists in recent years, has some excellent advantages, particularly for families with children. Without clinic responsibility now, however, I was free to move away from the mission center to live in closer proximity to the people I had come to love so dearly. It was amazing to think what God had done in my heart when He took me out of comfortable middle-class America and placed me in the midst of abject proverty and ignorance.

I found a house in Vertierres, a village on the main road, halfway betwen the OMS center in Vaudreuil and Cap Haitien. Though lacking many of the conveniences of the compound house, I soon felt cozily at home with a few of my own furnishings and collection of momentos which had a great deal of sentimental value.

"Madame Bonnette, Madame Bonnette, come quickly." These words were the first sounds to reach my sleepy ears one morning. Grabbing a robe I ran to the back door to see why Samson had awakened me in such a fashion. When I opened the door I discovered the reason. An old man with blood oozing from a large wound on his ankle was sitting on a bench.

My years as a nurse in Haiti had taught me to keep an emergency kit handy. It certainly paid off that morning. Samson ran for the kit as I applied a pressure compress with a dishtowel I had grabbed off the clothesline. It took a little time to clean the wound and dirty foot before applying medication.

Then I ran into a slight problem. I had found a hemostat and suturing material but no needle holder. I racked my brain trying to think of some way to improvise. Without a needle holder it would be very difficult to sew up the wound. Then inspiration struck! My tool box contained a pair of long-nosed pliers; sterilized in boiling water they served quite well.

While I sewed up the wound, the old man told me how the accident had happened. It seemed that while working in his garden a rock had rolled down the side of the mountain and struck his ankle a glancing blow. Someone had told him a few days earlier that a nurse now lived in the neighborhood. He had tied an old rag over the wound and hurriedly hobbled to my house.

This Hatian peasant, like so many others, was too poor to seek help at a hospital or clinic. He would either recover by using his own home remedies or die. Praise God this man recovered and faithfully returned each morning for new dressings and medication, listening attentively as we told him about Jesus.

The man was the first of a steady stream of people who started coming to my door. Somehow they always knew when I was awake. Each morning the little bench outside my back door was usually filled with waiting patients. There were old and young people, and sometimes a soldier from a nearby army post. Most often there were mothers with crying babies in arms trying to jiggle the cry out of them in typical Haitian fashion.

There was the usual assortment of ailments--colds, small cuts, headaches, worms, diarrhea. One teenage girl came with large blisters on her chest. Hot milk had been splashed on her. A woman arrived with blood streaming from a large cut on the side of her forehead. It seems she had been squating alongside a road, using the ditch for a latrine when a truck careened by knocking her over. Her head had been badly injured by a rock. Well, they all needed a little TLC and for me there was never a dull moment.

I began to acquire the needed medical supplies and planned an itinerary for my outstation clinics, to our more inaccessible churches in the northern and western parts of Haiti. As I prayed and sought guidance from the Lord, asking Him where He would have me begin the new ministry, I sensed Him nudging me in the direction of Du Pin, one of our remotest churches far beyond Ti Bois, where I had had my first unforgettable outstation experience.

As God blessed my ministry in Haiti, there came additional sweet confirmations that my daughter was also in the center of His will. Not only was Sidney enjoying Asbury College and growing in her faith, she had met and fallen in love with Bob Biddulph, the handsome young son of Burt and Bernardine Biddulph, OMS missionaries in Colombia. Burt, an outstanding evangelical leader in Latin America, had headed Colombia's Evangelism in Depth campaign and was the OMS field director there. The Biddulphs later pioneered the mission's work in Spain before returning to assist our Confraternidad Church in Bogota.

Bob and Sidney were married on December 20, 1969, in Wilmore, Kentucky, where Asbury College is located. I flew home for the ceremony which was held in the seminary's beautiful Estes Chapel. Burt and Dr.

Yippee in my Soul!

David Seamands, popular pastor of the Wilmore Methodist Church and now the famed author of *The Healing of Memories* and other best-sellers, officiated. Bob and Sidney were both sensing God's call to missions and would soon be appying to go to Spain with OMS.

Chapter Twenty-One

Journey To Du Pin

As I continued to pray about my outstation ministries I felt increasingly certain that the Lord wanted me to begin in the village of Du Pin. To reach Du Pin, located in the remote areas of western Haiti, required a strenuous trek up over several mountains. Since there are no proper roads and even footpaths at times are uncertain, it would be necessary to find a local man to serve as our guide.

As I planned the arduous journey I kept thinking, "How will I ever make it?" I'd just returned from furlough, a year in which I'd driven nearly 30,000 miles between speaking engagements. After all that sitting, I was anything but in shape. Yet God kept saying that He would be my strength. "Okay, Lord," I said, "this is your body and you are going to strengthen it. Everything's in your hands. Lead on."

My new jeep had not arrived from the States yet so I drove an old pickup to Hostin two days before the scheduled date for departure to Du Pin. Mémé, my Haitian nurse assistant, and I immediately began preparations. First thing we needed was a guide. That very day the Lord brought Pastor Julienne across our path, the very man who had invited me to Ti Bois, where the Lord had begun to burden me for the outstation ministry. We knew immediately that he was the one God had chosen. I realized, however, that Du Pin is a great deal farther than Ti Bois, and asking Pastor Julienne to travel that far with us was something of an imposition, yet he did not hesitate a minute. "O Madame Bonnette," he said, "it would be a privilege and a blessing to go with you to the place where God is calling." That was another confirmation that God was indeed leading us on. I also placed Pastor Julienne in charge of locating horses for us to ride plus another to carry supplies.

The day of our departure dawned beautiful and clear. All of us had had a good night's sleep and were raring to go. We met Pastor Julienne at our little Galilean Medical Center in Hostin. He had some bad news. All attempts at renting horses had failed. His sixteen-year-old son, however, had heard of the possibility of one horse. If successful, he agreed to meet us with the animal at Ti Bois atop the first mountain to be climbed in our journey to Du Pin. Before starting, the three of us knelt and Pastor Julienne led us in prayer asking God for continuous guidance, thanking Him for all He had done and for the ministry He was preparing for us.

In a little more than an hour we had traversed the plain and had begun the hike up the mountain. Before long my heart was beating rapidly. I was forced to call more and more frequently for short stops to recover my breath and strength to continue the climb. It occurred to me that when Moses walked through the desert those 40 years he had used a staff. If it was good enough for Moses, I thought, then it might be good enough for me. A stand of bamboo came into view and I asked a passing Haitian to cut a pole for me. It was amazing how much that bamboo cane helped shove me onwards and upwards.

About noon we arrived at Ti Bois. I flopped on the ground under a shade tree to recoup my energies. The temperature was a muggy 98 degrees, and my clothes were so wet I think I could have wrung out a quart of sweat. But it is never too hot to drink Haitian coffee. They served it to us just right--thick, black, mellow and laced with lots of brown sugar.

While Pastor Julienne went looking for horses Mémé and I drank coffee and chatted with the local people. I had brought along some soy bean seeds which I distributed to the church members. If Johnny Appleseed could do it so could I. Soy beans are a wonderful source of protein and I was interested to see whether or not they would grow in that area.

Pastor Julienne managed to rent a horse. "Madame Bonnette," he said, "you ride the horse and we will walk." I thanked the Lord for this provision, but after a look at the wooden saddle I wondered which would be worse, walking or riding! A chair was brought to help me mount. Even with the chair it took two men assisting to get me into that rough wooden frame. Now I had to learn Haitian horse language. I only knew two words--"whoa" and "giddy up." That wouldn't do for this animal. But soon I was yelling in Creole "La!" which means to stop and "Oui!" the signal for go.

I should mention here that tough as it is riding a Haitian horse, it is far harder to ride a Haitian donkey. I had heard about these animals and had promised myself I'd never get on one. One trip, however, I was so exhausted I think I would have ridden just about anything. Soon the pastor produced a donkey, placed a blanket on its back and helped me aboard. We had gone about 100 yards when that donkey just sat down. The pastor said, "That's all right, Madame Bonnette, he'll get up." Sure enough, he did and I climbed aboard again. But another hundred yards or so and he plopped down again. "Don't worry, Madame Bonnette," the pastor assured me, "he'll get up" and sure enough he did. I mounted him a third time and we continued.

We hadn't gone more than a block's distance when I overheard someone behind me whisper "Pastor, I think she's too fat for it." Humiliated, I got right off the donkey and walked the rest of the way. I consoled myself by recalling that Balaam's donkey had talked to him. At least my donkey had spared me that insult. Anyway, in Haiti horses have it all over donkeys!

Riding that horse wasn't so bad while traveling along the crest of the mountain where it was fairly flat, but when we arrived at the edge I gazed with apprehension at the tiny ribbon-like river far below. The steep, uneven footpath didn't look safe enough for a horse, let alone a horse with a rider, namely me! So much for riding. I decided I trusted my own feet rather than the horse's.

Down, down, down we went. My toes felt as though they were coming through my sneakers and clawing at the earth in an effort to break the descent. One slight misstep could have sent me tumbling over the side. I'm sure the angels were out in full force to keep me from falling. They've had to protect me many times in the past on some crazy venture. "Thank you, Lord, for the guardian angels," I prayed. Later I found that three toes on each foot were badly bruised. I solved the problem however by cutting the toes out of my sneakers!

Finally we reached the valley. What had looked like a tiny ribbon from above turned out to be a beautiful stream of cool, swift water. It took us only seconds to pull off our shoes and wade right in. So what if our clothes got wet. They were already soaked with perspiration. For a moment I thought how easy it would have been to stay right there for awhile and then forget about Du Pin and go back home. But the Lord was leading and we still had several mountains to climb before reaching our destination. Suddenly I felt as though I was being infused with a strange new sense of strength and vigor. I'll never be able to explain what happened, but when we resumed the journey again I had energy to spare.

I rode the horse or walked the next five hours up

and over, up and over each mountain. I'd sing "Onward Christian Soldiers" when on the horse, but when walking and too short of breath to sing, my spirit nevertheless kept repeating "Because He lives I can face this mountain."

Walking for hours does give one time to think. Conversation is hard, but the thinker doesn't stop. I thought of my lovely daughter and her husband, Bob Biddulph. Sydney had given birth to a beautiful baby girl whom she named Allison--my first grandchild. Now they were missionaries in Spain with OMS. My thoughts wandered back to the previous furlough and visits to friends who had so faithfully supported my ministry in Haiti. One family had taken me and a Haitian pastor to the St. Louis Zoo. What a wonderful day that had been. Then I remembered my favorite foods--yummy, junk food and especially moon pies. I even made a game out of trying to remember in order each church where I had spoken and each home where I had stayed while on furlough. I had to backtrack sometimes, but I believe all were remembered and prayed for. Somehow I am sure that when we get to heaven there will be no unfulfilled desires, no space or time limitations. When I want to see my friends--Bill and Joanne Whale for instance--they'll be there and we won't have to hurry our conversations.

There were times when I'd actually laugh out loud. Like the time I remembered a church in Texas where Dee Rucker, wife of our regional director, Carl, had introduced me as the motorcycle missionary and had my helmet there to prove it. She had sneaked it out of the trunk of my car. Wow! It would have been nice to be able to use my Honda on this trip, but I was reminded again of the impossibility as we scaled a rocky ledge that snaked along the side of the mountain.

Chapter Twenty-Two

A Night To Remember

Finally, at 5:00 p.m., after five hours of rough hiking, we neared Du Pin, a village located on one of the highest mountain ranges in that part of Haiti. We had passed the ruins of an old French fort said to have been built in 1802. Along the footpath I was surprised to see zinnias as they do not usually grow wild in Haiti. I wondered if a passer-by, perhaps a missionary, had years earlier scattered seeds along the trail. I still had some soy bean seeds, which I planted at random in the area. Hopefully they would grow and thrive and provide food for the Haitians for generations to come.

Soon the church came into view. The concrete block sanctuary with a corrugated tin roof had been erected by a work crusade a few years back. Nearby were two Haitian thatch huts. Only two? Had the Lord sent us all the way up here to minister to a mere handful of people. The next morning, however, we were in for a surprise. News of our arrival had travelled fast.

The sky clouded over as we made the final ascent.

We had no more than arrived when the heavens opened. This made it impossible for Mémé and me to set up our tent. The pastor, Brother Joseph, and his wife quickly vacated one room of their two-room home for us. This served as our bedroom and medical supply center for the duration of our stay. That night our guide, Pastor Julienne and his son, slept in a nearby hut.

I unpacked the rice, beans, cooking oil, and different seasonings. All of this when properly blended resulted in the most savory recipe of rice and beans, really delicious and satisfying. One of the local women volunteered to be our cook.

Mémé and I made up our beds and organized our belongings while supper was being prepared. I had brought only two sheets thinking we'd sleep together in the tent. Now we had only one sheet apiece. The room had two cots with but a single mattress. This was no problem, however, since I had brought along my inflatable air mattress.

Now to wash up before it got dark. No problem there either, as it was pouring down rain. We just stood outside and let the downpour cleanse body, soul, and clothes all at the same time. It was a cold rain, but after walking all day in the hot sun the chill felt good.

Supper was ready by the time we had changed our clothes. The four of us finished off a huge pot of rice and beans. Our dessert was bread dipped in coffee sweetened with generous doses of brown sugar.

Yippee in my Soul!

By then it was 7:30 and we were ready for bed. What a day! We blew out our little tin-can kerosene lamp and settled down for sleep. My prayer that night was a great big "Thank you, Lord."

But getting to sleep was not all that easy. I had slept in Haitian huts before, but this was something else. That night not only did we have the usual problems with bugs and rats, but an added and novel discomfort--bone penetrating cold. No one had told me it could get that cold anywhere in Haiti. Our flimsy sheets did not begin to keep us warm so we put on more clothing. Praise the Lord I found a nylon jacket in my pack; then I wrapped my feet in baby diapers we had brought for layettes. Swaddled in jacket and diapers I was finally drifting off to sleep when the invasion began. Rats! They infiltrated through the open ceiling rafters and ran down the side of the walls and over our beds in search of food. Fortunately we had stashed everything in our luggage or tupperware containers so their forays were unsuccessful. But the little beasts were definitely in a party mood, and they played tag all over that tiny room, squealing with delight when they caught each other. When I turned my flashlight on them they would scurry away but would soon slink back. I used that flashlight all night long. No sleep, but I learned a lot about rats!

Dawn came at last and both the rain and rats dispersed to be replaced by blue skies and bright sunshine. Now, Mémé and I did a switch. Instead of putting on clothes for the day we took off a few garments. We laughed at each other as jackets, blouses, and uniforms came off. To this day when I tell Haitians about how cold it gets in Du Pin, they don't believe me.

At breakfast I gave Pastor Julienne a narrative of our night's experience describing how the cold and rats had kept us awake most of the night. He looked puzzled informing us he had had a perfect night's rest--no problem with either cold nor rats. In fact, he said, two rats snuggled down and slept on top of his belly most of the night. I wondered if I could ever grow accustomed to rats as those dear people had. I doubted it.

Now it was time to head for the church and the beginning of our clinic day. During the night word of our arrival had spread throughout the region and to our amazement the little church was packed with people of all ages.

Chapter Twenty-Three

"I Did It! Praise God I Did It!"

Following a full 45 minutes of exuberant singing as only Haitians can sing Pastor Julienne brought a message. While he was preaching a wrinkled granny ran over to a friend, pointing a bony finger at the back of her shoulder where a plump bedbug reposed. A sharp swat took care of that. Granny then scratched the area several times. Now that's friendship! A few minutes later a youngster jumped out of his chair and dropped his drawers. Several adults came to his aid, located the offending bedbug and squashed it. Life must go on even in the midst of a service. When the invitation was given one woman raised her hand for prayer. Later that day she accepted Jesus as her Savior.

Mémé and I gave some instructions in simple health care and hygiene. Even the most basic concepts were unknown to them. We also distributed little greeting card sewing kits which women's groups in the U.S. had made. The rest of the morning we vaccinated 190 people for tuberculosis, took a ten-minute coffee break and then began examining patients.

No time for lunch, but we had another coffee break with bread at about three in the afternoon. The kids loved the tiny plastic cars we had brought. We were told that many had never before seen a toy. We finished consulting with the last of the sick at 5:00 p.m. It had been another full day. I prayed that we would see many of these sweet, wonderful people in heaven where they will be forever free of suffering.

Right after we finished eating it began raining again. Utterly exhausted I bundled up against the cold and managed to sleep peacefully through the first half of the night. But then began the same carnival of rodents as the night before. Several times a rat would try to get at my feet, but my trusty flashlight or a few swift kicks would send him scurrying up the wall.

Now I discovered that my air mattress was losing air. I found it had been punctured by a wire on that old cot. It was as flat as a fritter by morning. Still I was grateful for at least a half night's sleep.

We awakened again to a bright sunny day. Mémé and I packed up the medical supplies while breakfast was being prepared. The menu this morning was large hunks of bread dipped in coffee. I don't think I've ever eaten so much bread as I did on that trip.

The name Du Pin means "some bread." Maybe that is why I ate so much of it. Hopefully we left a little Bread

Yippee in my Soul!

of Life there.

     Now it was time to leave. As we said our goodbye to the folk in the neighborhood that same yippee which tickles my insides every time I've seen the Lord's manifestations was there. My whole being was full of adoration and thanksgiving for His great love that had guided us to that place.

     Pastor Julienne had managed to locate another horse. Off we rode into the sunrise in high spirits. That is, until we started our descent. Again I decided I preferred my own feet to those of the horse's. But every once in a while I'd climb back onto the saddle. Occasionally the nails would come loose and we'd have to take the saddle off, find a rock and pound everything back together again.

     At this time there were two single women, Robyn Cooper and Lollie Vitoria at the Hostin Medical Center, and in the past I had made my home with them while working in that area. When we arrived in the town I ran up toward the clinic shouting, "I did it. Praise God, I did it!" I'm sure they thought I was crazy before, and one look at me proved it. I was a dirty, stringy-haired, foot-weary, saddle-sore mess, but oh that "yippee" was still welling up inside of me.

     Pastor Julienne, his son, Mémé and I formed a little circle and prayed thanking the Lord for His protection for the journey. Heaven alone would reveal how the Holy Spirit had worked during that time at Du

Pin. We had only followed His orders leaving the results to Him.

One month later we returned to Du Pin. I immediately told the pastor that my assistant and I would sleep in a tent which we had brought. "Oh, no," he replied, "I have a cat to sleep with you. You'll have no trouble with rats now."

So back to the mud hut we went. Sure enough Pastor Joseph brought the cat in and tied it to a leg of the cot. Later I made sure no rats bothered us by having the cat sleep on top of my cot at my feet.

The next day I learned that that dear pastor had walked all the way down the mountain to buy the cat. Since that day I've had a special appreciation for felines and for that dear pastor who so sacrificially served us in a most practical way.

Years were spent ministering to our churches in the mountains of Haiti. Remembering that as Christ sent His disciples out two by two I always took an assistant, usually Mémé, with me. Traveling over the country's barren, rocky, treeless mountains we followed steep, narrow trails hardly wide enough for a donkey. If we met someone coming up or down it was every man for himself. At times I barely managed to scrambled out of the way. It was either get out of the way or go over the mountainside. On a few occasions when I decided to walk instead of ride, the horses had slipped and fallen into a ravine. Each time we were able to recover the animals, but lost some of the supplies, thanks to a few "helpful" Haitians. Oh, well, "c'est la vie" (that's life) as we say in Haiti.

Upon returning from the mountain churches I'd always go by the mission compound to pick up mail and learn the latest happenings. Missionaries Os and Kathy Heinrich's home was usually my first stop. After the mountain treks, sitting down at a table and using an inside bathroom were amenities I could really appreciate. Their loving friendship and Kathy's marvelous cooking always refreshed my body and soul. During their years on the field literally hundreds of people were blessed by their gift of godly hospitality.

Chapter Twenty-Four

"*This Is Where I Want You*"

In 1983, following a year of furlough, I returned to Haiti for my fifth term. I enjoyed the outstation ministry so much, but I felt God was leading me to build a house and clinic and establish my headquarters in some remote mountain area where people were so desperately in need of medical help. Of course, I would locate in the vicinity of a church so patients who came to the clinic could be properly evangelized and shepherded.

The field committee approved my request and also authorized me to replace my worn-out jeep with a pickup. During furlough I funded a rugged four-wheel drive half-ton Isuzu with an open bed in back. Someone had given me a fancy horn that played 64 tunes. Our missionary, Dave Shaferly, who can do just about anything, installed it and when I entered a village for a clinic or a child evangelism service I'd blow that horn and kids would come running from all over. They loved that horn!

It was agreed that on my return to Haiti I'd locate

at the mission guest house (called the Villa) at Port-au-Prince until I found a suitable location for my work. Since the main OMS clinic is in the north, I felt I should select a site in the southern mountains closer to the capital city.

For several weeks I traveled up and down the mountains trying to locate a suitable site to build a house. One day as I walked up an incline 16 miles inland from the nearest highway it was as though a voice said to me, "This is where I want you." It was a beautiful setting, surrounded by picturesque mountains. One could see the ocean and the city of Port-au-Prince in the distance.

Once the decision was made, one of our missionaries, Clyde Bowman, bulldozed a road up to the building site and leveled off the top of the ridge. A few weeks later an MFM work crusade consisting of six men and two women arrived to start the building. These work crusades are comprised of laymen from the U.S. and Canada who travel to the fields at their own expense contributing their skills and energy to the cause of missions. Through the years MFMers have built scores of homes, churches, schools, clinics, and camps all over the world.

Dave Shaferly directed the team and soon cement began to flow. Concrete blocks became walls and then a roof was poured. All of this was accomplished despite daunting obstacles. For instance, cement, sand, cement blocks, steel rods, nails, etc., had to be hauled up that treacherous mountain road. Water was transported in my pickup from the spring a mile away or sometimes carried in buckets on top of the heads of Haitian women.

A few weeks later another work crusade poured cement floors and then installed windows, doors, kitchen cabinets, plumbing, cisterns, and septic tank. Water from the cistern was hand-pumped to barrels on top of the house. There, by gravity, flow water ran down to the kitchen and bathroom. There was no electricity, but kerosene lamps provided adequate illumination at night. Since my house was the largest and most imposing in the area, I decided it was best not to paint the outside. The team did a beautiful job inside, painting every room a cheerful white.

While the men kept busy with construction the women were assigned the cooking. A full day's work created some tremendous appetites, and I knew these Western men would expect meat and potatoes at least once in a while. Most of our groceries had to be hauled from the city up the narrow mountain road. That was my job, driving the Isuzu loaded with building supplies as well as groceries. Instead of coffee breaks, the men had coke and fruit breaks. This required my keeping cases of cokes on hand, and Americans can't be expected to drink warm cokes so every third day I'd go down the mountain for large hunks of ice. Some food, however, could be obtained at the local open-air market. Here I could buy rice, beans, cornmeal, fruit and goat meat every day. In Haiti goat meat is really a staple. We gave them all sorts of sauces made with goat meat although it was awhile before the MFMers knew what kind of meat they were eating! Another mainstay was chicken. All chickens were bought live. Since there was no refrigeration, they were killed when ready to cook.

Working with those MFM crusades often furnished us with good laughs. One night one of the ladies needed to use the "bathroom." Not wanting to awaken the rest of the team she slipped out to the bushes. Amid unfamiliar surroundings she became confused. Groping around in the darkness she was soon thoroughly lost. She panicked and began yelling for help, but to no avail. Completely exhausted, every one of us was sleeping soundly. Finally a neighbor hearing her screams of distress found her wandering around in his cornfield and went to her aid. He recognized her as one of the whites working with me and shepherded her back to my house. When we learned what had happened we burst out laughing, but she couldn't make up her mind whether to laugh or cry!

During the building process I lived in a small trailer near the site and began to hold clinics, child evangelism classes and a Bible study. Once the doors and windows were installed, however, it was time to move in. Living with me in my new house was Sultamene, my new Haitian nurse assistant. What a God-send she was. I could not have begun to see the number of patients I did without her efficient help.

Sultamene was a beautiful, mature Christian woman, and we were united in spirit from the start. Basically quiet and soft-spoken, she underwent an amazing personality change the moment she stood up to tell people about the Lord. Bold and zealous she was as animated as any charismatic evangelist. People loved her and through her many came to accept Jesus as their personal Savior.

Samson, the Haitian boy that I had all but raised, would also come to be with me during the summer vacation and other holidays. He was living near Cap Haitien and studying at a mechanics training school. I always put him to work. He was good at household repairs and loved to work alongside Sultamene and me whenever we held clinics. He had learned to play a guitar and this was a real aid in evangelism and children's work. Sometimes I would find him under a tree playing his guitar to a group of young teenagers. He would teach them some Christian songs and pretty soon the valleys would vibrate with their singing.

A couple of other Haitians completed our little team. A seventeen-year-old girl, Solange, was my cook. When she first started working for me she could make only Haitian food, but after I had trained her she developed a wonderful proficiency in American cooking. I hired a part-time watchman, and he lived in a small Haitian hut at the edge of my property. It was his job to watch for prowlers at night and keep an eye on the house when I was away for clinics or trips into Port-au-Prince.

I soon began to discover the joys of simple living without so many of the machines and "conveniences" that clutter up our American way of life. Not having electricity to run a washing machine, I arranged with a Haitian woman to do my laundry. She would wash the clothes in a nearby spring, pounding them out on the rocks, and then spreading them in the hot sun to dry. The tropical sun would bleach my uniforms a beautiful white.

A visiting team from Indiana decided that, isolated as I was from the civilized world, I must have some means of communication, at least in the event of an emergency. Our missionary, Claude Beachy, rigged up a solar panel on my roof to provide electricity which charged a car battery giving me sufficient power to operate a short-wave radio. Claude even installed an electric light which I could run off the battery when it had sufficient juice. That was a real luxury although I rarely used the light in order to conserve the power for communication. Kerosene lamps do not provide the best illumination for reading, but I discovered if I put three lamps together on the table they were almost as bright as an electric bulb.

Without the distraction of television and some of the other accouterments of our Western way of life, it was easy to go to bed about nine and rise about six. I never knew when I would be called out of bed in the middle of the night to attend a patient. Sultamene, my assistant, would always meet the Haitians who came to our door during the night hours attending to them as she was able. If they needed assistance beyond her skills, she would knock gently on my door and call me out of bed.

The nearest church to my home and the clinic was in Léger, just two miles away. MFMers helped construct a cement block sanctuary. The Sunday school class and I poured the cement floor. Finding sand for the cement was always a problem. At times we had to haul it from Duvalierville, some 35 miles away. We did, however, eventually find a pocket of sand nearby. The Haitians would shovel it into bags, and then donkeys would haul it over the footpath to the main road where they would load it into the bed of my Isuzu for me to cart to the building site.

Since OMS had bulldozed the road to my new house, the government assumed no responsibility to maintain it. At times it got into an horrendous condition, but thanks to the efforts of our missionaries, Bill Glace and Clyde Bowman, who would come around with the bulldozer to periodically grade it, I was able to commute back and forth from our village to the main highway.

Chapter Twenty-Five

"*Jesus Was There*"

One afternoon a twelve-year-old boy showed up at my house with a badly mashed toe. I had to remove the toenail before applying any medication or dressing. He was so grateful for the relief from pain that he offered to cut the weeds in my yard. Of course, a machete is the lawnmower in Haiti. His name was Tinobe, and I developed a special affection for this energetic, bright faced little boy. Almost every morning he would show up to ask, "Madame, what can I do for you today?" Sultamene and I took every opportunity to talk to him about the Lord. He began to go to church with us and then one Sunday morning he knelt down to ask Jesus to come into his heart. Now, more than ever, he insisted on showing his gratitude by running errands for me. He practically lived at my house, delighting in doing odd jobs for me or at the church.

"Tinobe," I said to him one day, "how would you like to come and live with me. You can sleep in my medicine supply room at night." His face beamed with excitement. "Oh, Madame," he said, "I'd love to. Yes, I would really like to live with you."

We got permission from Tinobe's parents and he moved in. Later he told me his parents were voodoo worshippers and that they were only too happy to see him live at my place so they wouldn't have to feed him.

Tinobe was a joy to have around, but sometimes his enthusiasm created problems. He was constantly scouring the community and bringing people for me to treat. I told him that he didn't have to "drum up business" because there were enough patients coming to keep us plenty busy.

Between bulldozings, the road from my house half way down the mountain had to be maintained. It was only one lane and often blocked by landslides during the rainy seasons. One of Tinobe's jobs was to recruit a crew of workers. This was no problem for Tinobe since he was well-known in the community and had no trouble putting together a crew of men, women, and kids that he knew. They almost made a game of the work as they chanted African songs while they shoveled the site to the accompaniment of two youngsters beating out rhythms on bamboo poles.

One day Tinobe brought his friend, Benouir, to the clinic. "Benouir," he explained to me, "has worms and his parents will not give him money for medicine." Tinobe also had been talking to his friend about Jesus and told me that Benouir wanted to be converted. That is one of the sweetest memories I have. The two boys knelt with me and Benouir asked forgiveness for his sins. Then his little face lit up like a Christmas tree as he became a child of God.

Several weeks later a boy named Bouchtok, the son of the local witch doctor, came hobbling to the house with chic disease in both feet. The only cure was to dig out each chic flea, dislodge the eggs and then treat the infection. I had dug out about 20 of the fleas when Tinobe said, "Madame Bonnette, let me do that for you. I did it before for my brother." Tinobe didn't like my dental pick and asked for a large safety pin. We counted over 100 chic fleas extracted from Bouchtok's feet. From that time on Tinobe became my chief chic disease surgeon.

Since many Haitians have no shoes, we always kept cheap flip-flop sandals in different sizes on hand for patients with foot problems. Bouchtok was so thankful to have a pair of shoes that he promised to come each day for treatment and to keep them on until his feet were completely healed. Tinobe and Benouir became real friends to the witch doctor's son and before long Bouchtok too had received Christ. Now I had what I called my three musketeers. Those boys became great friends, almost inseparable except when one was called away by his parents to help work in the garden. They went with me on outstation clinics and to other mountain churches and were constantly recruiting kids for Sunday school. I sent all three of them to school with new pants, shirts and shoes. Sometimes they'd ask Sultamene or me to help them with reading or arithmetic. As their reading progressed I gave each of them a New Testament in the Creole language. We began having Bible studies together twice a week. I'd have each one read a few verses or a chapter and then say "Now, you tell me in your own words what you have just read." It was beautiful to hear each of them try to explain what Jesus was saying.

Shortly after I started my ministry in this mountain area I was saddened and disburbed to see so many babies brought to us with tetanus. Since neither Sultamene nor I could walk long distances over the mountains to deliver babies we sent out word that when a baby was born that the family should bring the infant to us with the placenta still attached. We would cut the umbilical cord using sterile technique and then gave them a layette set. The plan was a great success and regularly grannies, husbands, brothers or sisters would arrive having carried the newborn miles to get this service. I remember one little seven-year-old boy came carrying his newborn sister. When I asked where he lived he pointed at a mountain about two miles away as if to say, "Way over yonder." Praise God we never saw another tetanus baby.

Many Haitians named their children by the first word spoken right after the baby was born. Others gave them Biblical names such as Jean, Pierre, Daniel, Marie, or Miriam. Still other names were phrases that for some reason had special significance. I remember one woman who wanted to deliver her eighth baby at her sister's house some distance away. The day her labor began she commenced the long trek, but the baby had its own ideas. Before the woman was even a quarter of the way down the mountain the baby decided to enter the world right there on the trail. Two hours later the woman came carrying the baby to my house to have the cord cut. While I was working on the infant I asked if she had already named her. "Oh, yes," she replied. "Her name is "Jezu Té La" which means "Jesus was there." It was her way of expressing her thanks to her Lord who had seen her through the ordeal. As soon as the cord was cut and the baby attended to, that dear woman had to walk back to her home to prepare the evening meal. That was typical of the stark and grim character of life in Haiti. But in the midst of it all she had found peace and hope because "Jezu Té La"--Jesus was there.

Chapter Twenty-Six

"C'est la Vie"

Living entirely among the Haitians during these years and completely isolated from my Western friends, I had plenty of opportunity to observe Haitian society and culture. Haitian children are early taught a healthy respect for their elders. One afternoon when driving to the spring on a "water run" I passed some boys who waved me down and asked me for a ride. I was glad to oblige knowing that riding in my truck was a big treat for these youngsters. As we started up the hill I heard them holler "Stop, Madame, stop." The two boys jumped down and dashed towards the nearby house. As they approached a man appeared in the doorway. Suddenly the two boys dropped to their knees. "What's going on?" I asked Sultamene. "That man's their father," she explained. "They are asking his forgiveness for sneaking off. Let's see if they are forgiven or punished." In a moment the two boys got up and walked away evidently having obtained parental pardon for their sin.

Observing the diet of the Haitians I realized how

little variety they enjoyed. Every year they plant the same three crops--corn, beans, and sweet potatoes. Hoping to improve their diet I tried all types of vegetable seeds in my garden to see if they would grow in the area. If the results were satisfactory I'd give seeds or plants to the nearby villagers suggesting that they try. Within a short time I began to see cabbage, mustard greens, and carrots growing near their huts.

I once planted some white radishes in my garden. With the help of some liquid fertilizer, a gift from a friend in the States, they went berserk. Some grew as large as medium-sized watermelons. Tinobe loaded about 20 of the huge radishes in a wheelbarrow and took them to the local market. What a hilarious time he had! Most had never seen a radish, or any vegetable that size. "What is it?" they asked. Others wanted to taste this new vegetable. "How do you cook these things?" another woman asked. "Should they be boiled?" "Are they like potatoes?" asked another. "If you cut them in pieces and plant them will they grow new plants?" Tinobe and his radishes were the talk of the village for weeks.

One's diet could also be improved, I decided, by hunting some of the wildlife in the area. One day while driving down the mountain with my cook, Solange, I spotted four guinea hens ahead with what looked like some 50 baby chicks. "Look," I said braking the pickup. "Let's stop and see if we can catch some of those birds." This, I soon discovered, was easier said than done. Those elusive chicks scurried this way and that disappearing in the underbrush just when we thought we had them. They actually made fools of us as we ran back and forth searching under bushes and leaves. Finally, quite exhausted we managed to capture one which we took home.

As we finished our descent and approached the main highway, we narrowly avoided disaster. Rounding a curve, we met two speeding jeeps loaded with the fearful Ton-Ton Macoutes barreling right toward us. The president of Haiti, Jean Claude Duvalier, was driving the first jeep. I swerved just in time to avoid a head-on collision. I'm sure that I would not have lived to tell the story had I hit the president. The Macoutes had their machine guns in clear sight. Later I learned that the president often hunted guinea hens in that area.

Since Haitians eke out such a precarious existence, food is a most precious commodity and woe to any animal that invades a neighbor's garden. According to Haitian law in such cases it is permissable to wreak retribution on the animal, whether horse, goat, donkey or mule, with a machete. One afternoon a man appeared at my door with his recently chastised horse. There was a large machete gash on the animals right hip. I wished now I had taken a short course in veterinary medicine. Though we tied that horse's head to a tree he still managed to dance around and kick. I had just finished bandaging the cut when he broke loose and went crashing through my cornfield. In two minutes he managed to rip off the bandage and contaminate the wound that had taken me twenty minutes to treat. I finally used some horse sense and gave the farmer the medications and the bandages so he could care for the horse himself.

Treating animals became a part of my medical ministry. Each year all the dogs in that mountain range were brought to me for their anti-rabies shots. Having seen several children bitten by rabid dogs I was only too happy to give those injections.

Speaking of injections, Haiti abounds with a variety of quack doctors who call themselves "injectionists." They have no training, but somehow manage to get ahold of a 5cc glass syringe, needle, alcohol, penicillin and other medicines they can purchase over the counter from any pharmacy. The usual charge is $1 and this is negotiable. It is the general opinion that an injection will cure any ailment no matter what or where. Many times I received the handiwork of these irresponsible injectionists. Youngsters were often brought to us with huge abcesses on their buttocks or arms. One day a woman came to my house leading her blind husband. "Please, Madame," she implored, "please restore his sight."

"How long has he been blind?" I asked.
"One day," the woman replied.
"What happened?" I queried. "Did an injectionist give him shots in the eyes?"
"Yes, Madame. He said it would improve his vision."

I wanted to weep. Sadly I explained what the injectionist had done and that there was no medical cure, but I would pray for the man's healing. Both listened carefully as we explained the Gospel to them, but we never saw that couple again.

When the injectionist came by our place one day, Sultamene cornered the man asking him if he realized what harm and suffering he was causing. "C'est la vie" (that's life), he replied. "I'm just giving them what they want."

Tragedy is part of the warp and woof of life in Haiti. One evening a man was carried to my door, his body lacerated with ugly machete wounds from his head down to his knees. As Sultamene and I began to treat the wounds, we were told that a thief had broken into the man's house and he had awakened just as the door opened. As they struggled the thief lashed out with his machete. The wife kept screaming until some neighbors rushed over to investigate. Together they were able to overpower the intruder.

The Ton-Ton Macoutes arrived, took the captured burglar and marched him towards the nearest town. As they walked they beat the man about the head and body. Whenever he stumbled or fell they dragged him. He died about half-way down the mountain. The Macoutes just dug a hole beside the trail and dumped the body in it. No monument was ever erected over that grave. A desperate, too-brief life and a nameless grave seemed to somehow symbolize life for so many on this ruined and tragic island.

Chapter Twenty-Seven

Revolution!

On February 6, 1986, I drove my pickup down the mountain to the Villa, our mission house in Port-au-Prince. It was my birthday and I was going to celebrate it with Clyde and Marian Bowman, who were in charge of the Villa. I usually spent my special day with the OMS gang at our center in Vaudreuil in the north, 160 miles away, but our field director, Harold Brown, had radioed me to say there had been some riots in several cities between Port-au-Prince and Cap Haitien. He advised me to stay off the road if at all possible. In Port-au-Prince I went grocery shopping with Marian and bought some medical supplies. That night the three of us went out to a nice restaurant to celebrate my birthday.

The next morning we were awakened at four by the sound of gunfire. At breakfast our cook informed us that a coup d'etat had toppled the Duvalier government and Jean Claude Duvalier (Baby Doc) had fled the country with his wife. The reins of the government were now in the hands of General Namphy, a man of dubious character.

At the mission home in Port-au-Prince we had regular radio communication with the OMS center in Vaudreuil. Harold Brown warned us not to go outside the gate and instructed me to remain there at the Villa until it was judged safe to return to my home in the mountains.

For 30 years Haiti had endured the plunder and tyranny of the brutal and corrupt Duvalier family. Subsequent investigations revealed that one fifth of government income during their regime could not be traced. The family had bilked the country of an estimated 800 million dollars, and throughout this time the dreaded Ton-Ton Macoutes had conducted a reign of terror. Now, as word spread of the President's leaving, mobs began to form all over Haiti. Anarchy was the order of the day as homes were looted and burned and cars stolen. The large car dealership in Port-au-Prince owned by Baby Doc's father-in-law was looted and the automobiles stolen.

Special targets for revenge were the Blue Boys who had so long brutalized the people. Mobs crying "dechouke" (completely uproot and destroy) descended on the Ton-Ton's homes to plunder and kill. Commonly when they found the offender he would be decapitated and then his head paraded through the streets atop a bamboo pole.

We watched a mob form just outside our gate--at first just a few people calling for blood and "dechouke." But soon the numbers grew. They targeted a local

Macoute who was charged with putting names of neighborhood people on a hit list. At the last possible moment, marines arrived to rescue the man and take him away in a car. Several times a marine had to get out of the car and shoot into the air to discourage those hanging onto the vehicle. I must have jumped ten feet as a shot tore through our avacado tree sending a shower of leaves down into the yard.

For a week the Bowmans and I were restricted to the Villa. I made good use of that enforced vacation, spending extra time in the Word and prayer, and catching up on correspondence. I also had time to read some of my favorite Louis L'amour westerns. It was amazing how relaxing those western novels were, even when guns were going off all around us.

When things calmed down I was permitted to return to the mountains. On the way home I encountered only one road block on the main highway. "Thank you, Lord, for keeping me under your wings," I prayed as I began the climb up to Léger.

Sultamene, Solange and the "three musketeers" were at the house to greet me as I arrived. They had seen my little red pickup coming around the bend about a mile away and had gathered in front of the house to welcome me. They had no idea where I'd been those past seven days but had feared the worst. Of course, I had no way of contacting them. They said they had prayed for me constantly and that the Holy Spirit had assured them of my safe return. How often I thanked the Lord for my precious staff. We had become like a family bound by mutual love and dedication to common goals. Sultamene had carried on our medical ministry during my absence. She had also continued the Bible studies with the "three musketeers." What a faithful servant of God!

Due to the chaotic state of affairs in Haiti we thought it best to hire a regular watchman. This meant Tinobe had to give up his bed in the supply room and return to his parents' home. Still he was always around the house during the daytime. Senoumem, the new watchman, was a gentle, Christian young man, 26 years old. He stayed with us nights and was available in case Sultamene or I encountered problems.

We knew Senoumem was a zealous Christian when we hired him, but we soon discovered just how zealous. At night not only did he talk in his sleep, he preached in his sleep, though not in any language we could understand. He would emphasize a point by pounding on the wall beside his bed. Then he'd shout "Hallelujah! Hallelujah!" That we could understand! But to be awakened out of a sound sleep by his preaching was more than my assistant could take. She would get up and go to the supply room and pound on the door until the preaching stopped. Woe to any intruder who had ideas of breaking into my home. My watchman slept on the job but his nightly preaching seemed to bring down God's protective covering over the house.

With conditions so unstable and dangerous I was increasingly grateful for the means to communicate both with the Bowmans in Port-au-Prince and Mardy Picazo at the OMS center in Vaudreuil. I thank God for that group of MFMers who had supplied me with the short wave unit. In time, however, things died down and I hoped that life would proceed without any further disturbance.

Chapter Twenty-Eight

A Visit From The Kids

For a few weeks things did secm to die down. Up in the mountains, life went on very much as it had before the revolution. My daughter Sydney and her husband, Bob, with their three children had planned to visit me enroute to the U.S. from Spain, where they were completing their third term with OMS. I drove to Port-au-Prince and phoned them to say it was safe to come. What a joy a month later to see my little family arrive at the airport. My grandchildren, Allison, Philip, and Audrey, whom I had rarely seen, called me their "Grandma in Haiti." Now we would have time to get acquainted and they would see Grandma in action.

It was fun to watch my grandkids playing with the "three musketeers." Since the Haitian boys spoke only Creole I was afraid language would be a problem, but children have an amazing facility for communication, and soon they were playing happily even without a common language. Philip, the six year old, latched on to Tinobe. They spent many hours digging up sweet potatoes, cooking them over a charcoal fire, and feasting on the yummy results of their labors. The whole family loved Haitian food--rice and beans, goat meat stew, cornmeal mush, plus all the tropical fruits and vegetables.

Our calm interlude was coming to an end. Men from the plains again began to appear in the mountain villages to stir up trouble. We learned that they were being paid by communists determined to exploit the political instability of this period. The result was increasing anarchy, marked by mob rule and the breakdown of law and order. Anyone with a grudge seized the opportunity for retaliation. Angry mobs armed with clubs and machetes moved through towns and villages seeking victims and attacking on the least provocation. We began to witness in Haiti something very much like tribal warfare in Africa.

When the bloody forays ended Sultamene and I would get the results. The wounded from the opposing factions would trudge up to my house to wait forlornly in the yard for treatment. It seemed pathetically ironic that these same people just an hour earlier had been savagely attacking one another.

We spent many hours suturing machete wounds. One woman was brought to us with a gash across her back so deep that the shoulder blades and spinal areas were exposed. Though it appeared she had little chance of surviving, we spent two hours sewing up her wound and then gave her a large injection of ampicillin. After that, each morning Sultamene walked three miles to dress the wound and to give medications. Amazingly in a week the woman was strong enough to ride a horse to our house for further treatment. Daily we praised God for sparing her life. Once I asked her why she had been involved in the fight. "Well," she replied, "everyone else was." In a few months she not only delivered a healthy baby, but was walking--a feat which defies all medical explanations and can only be attributed to God's special mercy. During these turbulent times Sultamene and I stopped traveling to our outstation churches and ministered only at the house.

After two weeks my son-in-law had to leave for the States to fulfill some speaking engagements, agreeing that Sydney and the children would stay with me another month. The last few days things had calmed down and we hoped and prayed General Namphy had the country under control. We drove Bob to the Port-au-Prince airport. As we said our goodbyes I assured him that all would be well with the family.

It was time for Samson's summer vacation so I sent word to him to come down from Cap Haitien and meet us at a designated intersection. From there he would ride with us to my home in Léger where he would live with us for several months. Sure enough Samson was waiting there for us at the crossroads, and I witnessed a loving reunion between him and Sydney.

Encountering no problems, we bumped and swayed up the rough mountain road. Just a few miles from my house we passed a group of men with picks and machetes. On seeing our vehicle they suddenly came out of the field and started toward us. I sensed trouble and pushed the car up the steep rugged incline as fast as it would go. They began to give chase. I asked Samson to stick his head out the window and talk to them, hoping that seeing a Haitian they would let us alone. "What are you doing?" Samson yelled. The men paused a moment but then continued their pursuit. As they gained on us Sydney and I glanced worriedly at one another. We both recognized the immediate danger and also the need not to panic. We had the children to think of. By this time I was approaching my house and had to make a decision. If we stopped and took refuge in my concrete block home we would probably be safe, but undoubtedly all the luggage, food, and medical supplies in the truck would be stolen and the vehicle itself destroyed. My other option was to drive by the house and go on into the village to seek refuge at the home of Frère Ovid.

I had first met Frère Ovid years earlier when holding outstation clinics in Léger. Everyone called him Frère or father. He was, in fact, a Haitian layman who had never been ordained as a priest. "I have compassion on my people," he told me. "They've suffered so much. God sent me here to the mountains to help them. Like you, I too am a missionary." The local people called Frère Ovid their director and helped him build a large impressive church. They looked to him for guidance and council. In time, the Catholic church actually authorized him to perform marriages and give sacraments.

From the start, Frère Ovid had welcomed friendship with protestant missionaries. When Bill Glace was building the road to the village he made his headquarters at Frère Ovid's home. I often dropped by for a visit. Many times I talked to Frère Ovid about the Lord and the importance of a personal faith in Jesus Christ. Now in the absence of any possible protection from either the police or military, I decided to drive to Frère Ovid's house. I gunned the motor and we careened through the tiny village, skidding to a halt in front of the parsonage. We glanced back and were relieved to see that the mob had stopped at some distance although they remained there waiting, sullen and menacing. I jumped from the truck, ran into the house and quickly explained our situation to my Catholic friend. He immediately ran out to meet the mob. We don't know what he said but in a moment they dispersed. "Don't worry, Madame," he assured me. "I've talked to those men. They are not from this area and they won't bother you again." After a while we drove home thanking the Lord again and again for His overshadowing presence and for providing Frère Ovid.

For the next three weeks my daughter, grandchildren, and I had a great time getting to know one another. Some uprisings continued in the area but they were relatively minor and only a few wounded were brought to the house. We felt it prudent to venture out no further than the village market place and kept the kids near the house at all times. Samson had learned to play the guitar and entertained us with his music and crazy jokes. Sometimes when he played I'd accompany him with my snare drum. The hills around us vibrated with our songs and laughter.

Yippee in my Soul!

Finally it was time for Sydney and the children to leave for the States. As we traveled down to Port-au-Prince all was quiet until we turned down to the main street of the city. Suddenly we heard gun shots behind us. Within seconds the street, ordinarily two lanes, was jammed with five lanes of traffic, all headed in the same direction--away from the sound of gunfire. I took off on a side street as soon as possible and made it to our mission house. Later we learned that seven people had been killed just a half block behind us. "Praise God," I sighed. "Thank You again for escorting us out of the jaws of death."

Chapter Twenty-Nine

Farewell

Back on the mountain I continued the clinic ministry, but now I had the curious sensation that a phase of my life, my time in Haiti, was rapidly drawing to a close. The feeling had begun three months earlier. As I prayed, the Holy Spirit seemed to be telling me I would soon be leaving this country which I so loved. "Certainly not," I argued. "Haiti has been my home for 20 years. I love Haiti and its people and they love me. They need me, Lord; you know I'm planning to retire in Haiti. I can be happy up here on this mountain till the day I die."

As I thought of the prospect of leaving Haiti my future seemed clouded with uncertainty. "Lord," I argued, "what am I supposed to do next? I have no husband, no relatives to go to. My daughter is in Spain. What will I do?"

But pray and argue as I might, there came a growing and unshakable conviction that I must prepare to leave. "Your work in Haiti is done," the Lord seemed to be saying with unarguable finality.

Yippee in my Soul!

Now the violence, which had subsided, began to escalate again. These were the days of road blocks. Everywhere self-appointed vigilantes built barricades with logs, barbed wire and burning tires to stop all traffic in order to apprehend Macoutes or others on their hit lists. This then encouraged unscrupulous thugs to set up road blocks of their own to exact tolls from all who passed. Those who resisted were threatened, roughed up or worse. Practically every time I traveled anywhere I'd be stopped by road blocks. I used various devices to deal with these hoodlums. "Look, I'm a nurse," I'd say. "You let me through and when you get injured I'll treat you free of charge" or "I'm just a poor missionary and anyway I don't have much money, but let me give you this mango." And often a smile or a little good humoured banter was enough to get me through. But when these ploys failed there was nothing to do but grudgingly pay up. Thank God, in all my travels, He still kept me under His protective wings.

Now again the communists lackeys from the plains began to appear in the mountain areas, stirring up trouble. Night after night I heard prowlers around the house. I seldom got a full night's sleep. We began to find threatening notes tied to stones or placed in my driveway. Too dangerous to travel to outlying areas, I confined my medical work to my home in Léger. This however, allowed more time for Bible studies and discipleship training with my "three musketeers" and five adult Christians from that area.

I admit my heart was heavy that June as I made

preparations to leave my mountain home. Using the radio, I arranged with Clyde Bowman to drive his pickup to Léger the 23rd to transport the mission furniture and equipment to Port-au-Prince. I would follow with my stuff in my truck. The night before I'd hauled Sultamene's and Solange's belongings to their homes, waiting until it was late enough for local villagers to be asleep so as not to raise questions.

The next morning came one of the saddest partings of my life. Tears flowed as I embraced Sultamene, Solange, my three musketeers and Senoumem, the watchman. It was like leaving my own family. But deep inside I knew this was God's will and that I was being obedient to the promptings of the Holy Spirit. Though I was leaving, Jesus would remain in those mountains embodied in those precious co-workers whom I'd had the privilege of discipling.

The trip from Léger to Port-au-Prince was without incident. Now there came a feeling of relief. I was out of the treacherous mountain area and things in Port-au-Prince seemed calm enough. Later that day I drove to the home of a Haitian woman who had stored some of my valuables. All was quiet going to her house, but as I again entered the city the vehicle in front of me came to an abrupt halt. On the opposite side of the road a large military truck had stopped. About a dozen Leopards (a special army group similar to the U.S. Green Berets) jumped out and began pursuing a man standing near the side of my pickup. In a moment there were Leopards all around running and shooting. "Lord," I cried, "help! Get me out of this gunfire." Suddenly I was impressed to turn my wheel sharply to the right and drive up on the sidewalk. As I proceeded around the truck in front of me I heard a man scream, "No! No!" Then a gun shot. He fell over, mortally wounded. Once around the truck, the street was clear and I drove away at high speed. But I had gone only a few blocks before I was forced to pull over to the side of the road. For many years I had seen repulsive sights--diseases, wounds, maggots, ulcers. I had prided myself on my strong stomach, but now I was about to throw up. More than this, it was as though a great dam inside me had suddenly burst under the accumulated pressure of the past weeks. I put my head in my hands and wept and wept, the tears running down my face in torrents.

Back at the Villa the tears continued to flow. The next day was Sunday and I went to church with the Bowmans. I thought I had myself under control. After church we went out to eat. I had no sooner ordered when unaccountably I began to weep and weep. I couldn't stop. Clyde and Marian took me back to the Villa and then returned to finish their dinner. Throughout the next day tears were welling in my eyes especially as I boarded the Missionary Flights plane for West Palm Beach, Florida. I cried off and on throughout the entire flight.

Our director of field ministries and former Haiti field director, David Graffenberger, suggested that I stay with our friends, Marvin and Reba McClain, for some R & R. McClains were dear friends who had served in Haiti for a short term. Being with them would certainly provide a time of rest and recreation in an atmosphere permeated by loving concern. The next day when I met our MFM representative Harry Burr, I thought I had my emotions in hand, but I had no sooner begun to tell him about recent events in Haiti when I found myself again weeping.

I was at McClains only a short time before Reba confided that she was concerned about a lump in her breast. I insisted that she see a doctor immediately. The result was a masectomy, but too late, for the cancer had already spread throughout Reba's body. She died one month later. But I was there at that time by the Lord's appointment, I know now, not only to minister to the McClains, but in so doing to recover my own poise and find healing for the deep wounds that those final months in Haiti had left upon my own spirit.

Although I knew I would not be returning to Haiti, I spent a year and a half traveling to churches all over America sharing with them a record of God's faithfulness and protection in time of trouble. At the same time it was a joy to help raise support for our younger missionaries and other mission needs.

From 1988-90 I had the joy of being in Spain with Sydney, Bob and my precious grandchildren. It was a privilege to assist the OMS ministry on that field and I especially delighted in serving as camp nurse at our beautiful Pena de Horeb camp 40 miles north of the city of Madrid.

At the present time I reside at the Missionary

Yippee in my Soul!

Village in Bradenton, Florida. This, too, has been part of God's loving provision for me. The battle with Satan in Haiti is still raging, but every day multitudes of Haitians are coming into the Kingdom, and even in that darkened, impoverished, exploited, voodoo-ridden republic, God will win. I praise Him for the privilege of having had a part in sharing that reality. All those years of hardship, heartache and joy were more than worth it. He is worth it and the yippee is still in my soul!

If you would like to have Margaret Bonnette speak at your church, please write her at:

Bradenton Missionary Village
1200 Aurora Blvd.
Bradenton, FL. 34202

Or phone her at (813) 746-5092

APPENDIX
by Ed Erny

I.   A Brief History of Haiti

Haiti is the western one-third of the once-fabled island of Hispanola, discovered by Columbus in 1492. The Dominican Republic comprises the eastern two-thirds of the island.

Columbus, and the Spanish who followed him, brutally subjugated the Indians, coercing them to slave labor. So cruel and inhumane were they that this race of aboriginals was decimated and virtually disappeared. To fill the diminishing ranks of laborers, in 1530 the plantation owners began importing slaves from Africa to work the fields which provided sugar, coffee, sisal, and rum to the markets of Europe and America. In time (in the 16th century) Spaniards, however, began to abandon Hispanola for the more promising prospects of gold in Mexico and Central and South America. Now pirates from France, England, and Holland took over the island's coastal areas preying upon the gold-laden Spanish galleons which passed through the Caribbean waters headed for the North Atlantic and home. When the French influence

Yippee in my Soul!

became dominant in 1697, Spain recognized French control of the western one-third of Hispanola.

The French named the colony Saint Dominque, and so prosperous were the great plantations to the empire that France came to regard it as the jewel in the imperial crown, more lucrative than even Canada. By 1788 there were 500,000 slaves in Haiti, eight times the number of French residents of the island.

By 1790, however, the slaves were growing restless and there was talk of revolt. And no wonder, the plantation task masters pushed their chattel to the limit of their endurance, working them from dawn to nightfall, and frequently as late as nine or ten at night. Catholic holy days provided the only respite from this cruel routine, and plantation owners petitioned Rome to reduce the number of holy days which required observance in Haiti so as to get more work from their blacks. The average life expectancy of the negro on a Haitian plantation was ten years!

On the night of August 14, 1791, a large number of slaves gathered surreptitiously on the plain of Bois Caimen, and after a voodoo ceremony organized a revolt. The next day they proceeded to massacre scores of French.

Two things contributed to the unprecedented success of this uprising. First, slaves outnumbered the French eight to one. Still their victory would have been shortlived had not the outbreak of the rebellion virtually coincided with the French Revolution. The chaotic conditions of France made it difficult for the empire to respond with the usual draconian reprisals that such upstart rebellions had always provoked. Napolean did try to retake possession of Haiti in 1799, but his troops were decimated by yellow fever. By the year 1804 the slaves had triumphed. They named their new country, the first black republic in the western hemisphere, Haiti.

The political and economic history of Haiti, following its independence from the French, makes for dismal reading indeed. The black leaders who had engineered the slave revolt soon quarreled amongst themselves. For a time there was a civil war between the government in the South under General Petion and that of the North ruled by General Henri Christophe who built The Citadel, a huge, outlandish and imposing fort erected on a bluff overlooking the sea near Cap Haitien. (It remains the prime tourist attraction in Haiti today.)

The country was finally reunited under J.P. Boyer. During the next 70 years 32 different men ruled Haiti! By the turn of the century, so chaotic were conditions in Haiti that in the eyes of the U.S., the island seriously compromised the security of the entire hemisphere. As a result, in 1915 President Woodrow Wilson sent the U.S. Marines to Haiti to restore order. From 1915 to 1934 Haiti was, in effect, a U.S. protectorate. During this period remarkable headway was made in the areas of education, transportation, and commerce. After the U.S. withdrawal in 1934, however, the conditions deteriorated rapidly with the succession of army officers organizing coups and again seizing the reins of government.

In the first free election in the history of the nation, in 1957, a tough, rough-hewn country doctor by the name of Francois Duvalier was elected president. Upon his death, the reins of government passed to his son Jean Claude Duvalier, known as "Baby Doc." After Baby Doc's ouster in 1986, the country was run by a succession of military dictators until the election of Jean Bertrand Aristide in 1990. As of this writing Aristide is still President of Haiti.

II.   Voodoo in Haiti

Demon possession is but one facet of the evil voodoo religion that holds most Haitians in its thrall. Throughout Haiti one finds the voodoo witch doctors called Hungan. The famous (supposedly more powerful) of them demand exorbitant fees. But everywhere there are the small-time witch doctors who will settle for payment for their services in the form of a chicken, pig, goat or whatever small trinket they can get. They claim to possess powers to bring prosperity, a good harvest, put a curse on one's enemy, or heal diseases. Margaret remembers one woman who brought her baby to the clinic. She had first taken her to the local witch doctor. The man had declared that the only way to drive the spirit of disease out of the infant was with fire. He had lashed the infant to a spit and hung it over a flame just as one would barbecue a hunk of meat. She did survive but was horribly disfigured.

Appendix

To explain the hold that voodoo has over the Haitians, one needs to understand something of the history of this infernal religion. Voodoo is a combination or an intermingling of African cult religions with a debased form of Catholicism. In voodooism there are also traces of European folklore, Norman and Breton traditions, as well as Masonic rites. How did this all come about?

In the 17th century during the French occupation of the island, colonists began to import thousands of slaves to work the prosperous plantations. Most of these Africans came from the so-called slave coast area of Africa, the countries most largely represented being Dahomey and Nigeria. Anthropologists agree that a preponderance of Haitian slaves came from the Dahomey area. To appreciate something of the depravity of the African religion in Dahomey we need to know that at this time human sacrifice was still practiced on a large scale in that region. For sheer cruelty the King of Dahomey was virtually without rival. In the 17th century he smashed the Wydah nation and created what some have described as a great slave emporium. He systematically proceeded to sell thousands of his countrymen to the white slave traders in exchange for firearms, rum, and other western commodities. Every year he made a raid on other neighboring tribes to secure additional plunder in human flesh to sell to the slavers. For years this man sold them an average of 10,000 slaves a year.

In the eyes of the French the only moral justification for the heinous slave traffic was that by enslaving the blacks the Christians would then have opportunity to "convert" them.   In 1664 a police decree required that all French plantation owners in Haiti baptize their slaves, thereby, of course, "making them Christians." These same plantation owners, however, fearful that the slaves would acquire Christian notions of equality, were careful to prevent them from receiving religious instruction.   French priests were actually barred from many of the French plantations.   It should be remembered that just prior to the French Revolution, Christian religious faith in France had reached a nadir of debasement and degradation.   The French Revolution was as much a revolt against the Christian faith as it was against the aristocracy.   It is a well-known fact that at the outbreak of the Revolution the rabble of Paris desecrated the Notre Dame and others of the great cathedrals of France.   They actually enthroned a prostitute as queen in the Notre Dame cathedral.

What bits of Catholic ritual and religion the slaves did pick up were gradually incorporated into their own African cults.   Life for a Haitian slave was terrible to say the least, and for escape the slaves retreated at night to forest glades to practice their pagan cults.   A French writer, Moreau de Saint-Mery, in his book *Description of the French Part of St. Dominque,* describes the voodoo ceremonies which he witnessed.   He writes, "It is the snake god under whose auspices gather all who share the voodoo faith.   The snake will not give of its power or make known its will except through a high priest or priestess known as king and queen, master or mistress, or even papa or momman.   If the snake approves the admission of a candidate to the society, the sorceress sets out the duties that must be fulfilled. The priest receives the tribute and presents which he expects as his due. To disobey is to resist the god and insure misfortune.

"Voodoo gatherings take place secretly at night in a cloistered place, shut off from the eyes of the profane. The priest and priestess prepare an altar containing a snake in a cage. After various ceremonies the king and queen and all initiates approach in order of seniority and entreat the voodoo, telling him what they most desire. The queen gets onto the box in which lies the snake, a python, and she is penetrated by the god. She writhes, and her whole body is convulsed when the oracle speaks from her mouth. The snake is then put back on the altar and everyone brings it an offering. A goat is sacrificed and the blood is collected in a jar. It is used to seal the lips of all present with a vow to suffer death rather than reveal anything, even to inflict it on whoever might be forgetful of such a momentous pledge.

"Then begins what is strictly speaking the 'dnase vaudou'. This is the moment when new initiates are received into the sect. Possessed by a spirit, the novices do not come out of their trance until a priest hits them on the head with his hand, wooden spoon, or if he thinks necessary, oxhide whip.

"The ceremony ends with a collective delirium. Some are subject to fainting fits, others to a sort of fury, but with all there is a nervous trembling which apparently cannot be controlled. They turn round and round while they tear their clothes in this bacchanal and even bite their own flesh. Others merely loose consciousness, and falling down are carried into a neighboring room where in the darkness a disgusting form of prostitution holds hideous sway."

One of the African cults which the slaves imported to Haiti is the cult of the panther woman. According to a legend, in ancient Africa a baby girl was born as a result of a union between a panther and a woman. She then became the priestess presiding over the panther cult. Witnesses report that when possessed by this particular demon, the victim's arms stiffen and his fingers assume a claw-like form.

Alfred Metraux, a well-known anthropologist, who devoted much of his life to the study of Haitian voodoo estimated that in the 1940s more than 90% of Haitians practiced voodoo. At present although more than 25% of Haitians claim to be evangelical Christians, it is safe to say the great majority of Haitians are still deeply influenced by the voodoo religion, and sadly even Christians often retain their fear of voodoo influence and the powers of witch doctors. It is claimed that in the famous voodoo ceremony of 1791, which inaugurated the slave revolt, the country of Haiti was offered to Satan in perpetuity in exchange for deliverance from the French task masters.

Another phenomenon that is often associated with Haitian voodoo is that of the zombie. Though skeptics tend to write off zombies as myth and superstition, it is difficult to find a Haitian who does not put some credence in the existence of zombies. In a recent book entitled *The Serpent and the Rainbow* the author, who spent some time in Haiti, claims that practitioners of voodoo have concocted a poison extracted from the puffer fish (a culinary delicacy in Japan), which causes the victim, though still living, to assume a death-like state. After the burial of the supposed corpse, the victim is then exhumed, revived, and kept or sold as a zombie slave. Zombies are still able to speak, understand, and perform menial services for their masters while in a trance-like condition.

Alfred Metraux points out that Article 246 of the old penal code relates to the zombie as follows: "Also to be termed intention to kill, by poisoning, is that use of substances whereby a person is not killed but reduced to a state of lethargy more or less prolonged. This without regard to the manner in which the substances are used, or what were their later results."

Metraux goes on to say, "For the common people, zombies are the living dead--corpses which a sorcerer has extracted from their tombs and raised by a process which no one really knows. The spark of life which sorcerers wake in a corpse does not wholly give the dead man back his place in society. A zombie remains in the misty zone, which divides life from death. He moves, eats, hears what is said to him, even speaks, but has no memory and no knowledge of his condition. The zombie is a beast of burden which his master exploits without mercy, making him work in the fields, weighing him down with labor, whipping him freely and feeding him on meager tasteless food."

Yippee in my Soul!

I have shared the above to help the reader understand the depravity which is so much a part of this sad legacy of the nation of Haiti. When one hears of political corruption and economic chaos in Haiti, we need to remember the dark satanic depths that have been part of the history of this unfortunate people. We praise God for the inroads of the Gospel and the glorious light of liberty in Christ Jesus which is beginning to penetrate that dark culture and sets great numbers of Haitians free.